ALSO BY DOUG TAYLOR

Lilies of the Covenant

The trials and joys of five generations of the Taylor family, in eighteenth-century England, nineteenth-century Newfoundland, and twentieth-century Toronto.

Citadel on the Hill

A history of a church community in Toronto in the first decade of the twentieth century, chronicling the trials and successes of the congregation as it progresses into the modern era.

The Pathway of Duty

An immigrant family from England arrives in Canada in the early years of the twentieth century and struggles to survive in the harsh conditions of Toronto's Earlscourt District. The sinking of the *Empress of Ireland* in 1914, in the icy waters of the St. Lawrence River, dramatically changes their lives forever.

There Never Was a Better Time

Two young brothers immigrate to Canada. This is a humorous and intimate glimpse into their family life in bustling Toronto during the 1920s, as well as the adventures of their brothers, parents, and rascal of a grandfather.

Arse over Teakettle

An intriguing tale of growing up in Toronto during the days of the Second World War and the post-war years. Tom Hudson and his mischievous friend "Shorty" find adventure in their seemingly quiet neighbourhood, as they yearn to learn about the secrets of the older boys.

THE VILLAGES WITHIN

An Irreverent History of Toronto and a
Respectful Guide to the St. Andrew's Market,
the Kings West District, the Kensington
Market, and Queen Street West

DOUG TAYLOR

iUniverse, Inc.
New York   Bloomington

The Villages Within
An Irreverent History of Toronto and a Respectful Guide
to the St. Andrew's Market, the Kings West District,
the Kensington Market, and Queen Street West

iUniverse books may be ordered through booksellers or by contacting:

iUniverse
1663 Liberty Drive
Bloomington, IN 47403
www.iuniverse.com
1-800-Authors (1-800-288-4677)

Because of the dynamic nature of the Internet, any Web addresses or links contained in this book may have changed since publication and may no longer be valid. The views expressed in this work are solely those of the author and do not necessarily reflect the views of the publisher, and the publisher hereby disclaims any responsibility for them.

ISBN: 978-1-4502-2524-3 (pbk)
ISBN: 978-1-4502-2526-7 (cloth)
ISBN: 978-1-4502-2525-0 (ebook)

Printed in the United States of America

iUniverse rev. date: 8/31/10

The author dedicates this book to readers who might enjoy a satirical version of Toronto's early history and appreciate a non-academic study of its rich architectural and social history.

Contents

Prefatory Propaganda
Toronto—a Hell of a Town

"Toronto is a hell of a town." I offer these words with a sense of awe, aware that many Canadians would prefer to say, "Toronto *is* hell."

According to some of our national cultural gurus, complaining about Toronto is the true national sport, surpassing baseball, ice hockey, or even "mattress hockey" (in which high sticking is considered an asset). Others state that bitching about Toronto is the glue that binds our country together. Perhaps there is some truth to these ideas, as I have encountered Torontophobes from the Atlantic coast to the Pacific shores, their numbers exceeding the proliferation of Timbits strewn across the nation.

Canadians living beyond Toronto's borders decry its flat, boring landscape, oblivious to its verdant river valleys and the lofty heights of the Davenport Road hill, which sweeps across the city, providing impressive panoramas of the towering high-rises nestled around the shores of the lake. They seem unaware of the many forested streets and intimate neighbourhoods, tucked between the busy downtown thoroughfares. A short ferry ride from the skyscrapers of Bay Street, the Toronto Islands provide a recreational retreat that seems a world away from the city's bustling avenues. The Toronto landscape has much to offer a perceptive observer.

Critics state that Toronto traffic is murder, and that the Don Valley Parkway should be more appropriately named the Don Valley Parking Lot. The capacity of the Gardiner Expressway, they say, is stretched beyond the limits of the most generously proportioned girdle. During rush hours, Toronto's pedestrian traffic obstructs the city's sidewalks to the point that they are impassable. However, the crush of humanity is usually not a problem, unless it is an extremely hot day and deodorant is in short supply. Travelling on the subway is a noticeable exception.

Critics claim that Toronto's crime rates are devastatingly high, despite statistics proving it is one of the safest cities in the world. We suspect that the city's worst crime is claiming the title "The Nation's Largest Urban Centre."

Some complain that the litter on the streets of Toronto is knee deep and the waterfront is a disgrace—cluttered and sterile. The urban sprawl is endless, and the summer smog is suffocating. The depths of evil that haunt Toronto are amazing. Even more amazing is that many of the city's detractors have never set foot within its precincts.

They know that Toronto is a loser's town, as evidenced each week throughout the winter season on *Hockey Night in Canada*. Many Canadians state that Torontonians are too urbancentric, believing that their city is superior to all others in Canada. If only this were true. In fact, too many Torontonians complaint about the city's lack of this, that, or the other, constantly demonstrating that they possess very little urbancentricity. When something about the city displeases them, they cry, "Only in Toronto does ..."

Those who are actually proud of their city seem reluctant to express it publicly.

Another complaint from Torontophobes is that the city sucks vast fortunes from the federal government, to the detriment of other regions in Canada. They claim that they are able to hear the sucking noise as Toronto vacuums the cash from Ottawa and empties it into the vaults on Bay Street. However, it is more likely that the noise is the sound of government officials flushing Torontophobic ideas into the empty spaces between the ears of some of the members of parliament. Contrary to well-established scientific principles, in this instance, sound can travel in a vacuum.

If only it were true that Toronto receives too great a share of the government's largesse. On the contrary, Ottawa is convinced that giving anything to Toronto will deprive them of votes in the other regions of Canada. For example, recently declassified private papers of Prime Minister Pearson revealed that when his government was considering a Canadian submission for the 1967 World's Fair, the prime minister said that hell would freeze over before he would support a bid from Toronto. In another instance, when they held the final voting to choose the host city for the 2008 Summer Olympics, Ottawa was absent from the scene, and federal financing for the games had not been nailed down.

However, in 2009, when Toronto submitted its bid for the 2015 Pan Am Games, for the first time, the federal money was in place before the final voting. By coincidence, in that year the minority government of the day had concluded that the only path to a majority was through the voters of Ontario.

Prime ministers seem to fear that if they give anything to Toronto, the remainder of the country will punish their government at the polls. As if voters require a reason to punish any government that is located within a five-hour drive (contaminating distance) of Toronto. However, the myth persists that Toronto receives preferential treatment from Ottawa. Other provinces continue to accept federal money without much thought as to where the funds originate.

Ontario's economic output and the taxes it contributes are almost equal to the combined economies of Alberta and British Columbia. Imagine Ontario dumping all that filthy cash into the coffers of a land that is famous for its unspoiled waterways and virgin forests.

Due to the manner in which the federal government calculates the equalization payments, they recently have declared Ontario a "have-not" province. However, any money the province receives under this program will be derived from its own coffers. An odd arrangement indeed!

Ontario remains the cash cow of Canada, and Toronto is the cash cow of Ontario. Even with the vast oil resources of western Canada and the devastating effects of the recession on the manufacturing industries of Ontario, this continues to be true.

Another complaint is that Toronto is the only Canadian city that considers itself "world class." Really? The *only* city in Canada?

However, consider the following question. Is there any metropolitan area in the developed world the size of Toronto that the international community does not recognize as world class? Toronto's immense population and resources attract and sustain important cultural, industrial, scientific, financial, and educational institutions. It is home to over a hundred entities that the international community rates as being "world class."

This does not mean that the city is without problems or failings. If this were true, no city in the world would deserve such a designation. Toronto is the cultural and financial capital of the nation, and internationally recognized as one of the largest cultural scenes in the world.

The urban guru Richard Florida, author of *The Rise of the Creative Class,* rated Toronto as one of the most creative, diverse, and tolerant cities in the world. The Gay Pride Parade is one of the world's largest, and the gay community is not only tolerated, it is celebrated. In addition, each summer, ethnic neighbourhoods have their own festivals and their presence in the urban landscape is a source of pride for all Torontonians.

Yet many derogatorily refer to the city as "Hogtown," and some call it far worse names. Most are unaware of the origin of the term Hogtown, failing to realize that it was originally intended as a compliment. In the nineteenth century, Toronto was where farmers from the hinterland visited to "live high off the hog," not to be confused with politicians whose "snouts are in the trough," who are prolific in every century. Today, many residents of the city employ the nickname Hogtown affectionately.

In the nineteenth century, Toronto's motto was "The City of Laughter and Light." Paris was later to borrow a part of this slogan. However, even today, Toronto remains a great place to laugh and "get lit."

Recently, a beer company advertised that their brew was "colder than the residents of Toronto." This tongue-in-cheek commercial perpetuates another myth. It is true that in a large metropolis, people cannot smile and greet everyone they pass on the street. However, visitors to the city frequently comment on the friendliness of its citizens, because they readily respond to a smile or greeting. When a visitor is standing on a street corner holding a city map, people often ask if they can be of help. In the days prior to phone cameras, when Torontonians noticed people taking pictures they assumed they were tourists and readily inquired if they required assistance. This desire to be helpful remains evident today.

Hold open a door for a person or say "good morning," and most Torontonians will respond in a friendly manner. Toronto is a city where it is easy to converse with people you meet, if you are willing to take the time and make the effort. However, this does not apply during the evening rush hour. During this frantic time of the day, the populace turns carnivorous and devours anyone who impedes his or her journey homeward. In the morning rush hour, people are too comatose to respond to anything less than the detonation of an atomic bomb. However, if the TTC announces a delay on the subway, the heated reactions are sufficient to scorch the tiles of the underground stations.

It is rare to find a visitor from the United States, Europe, or Asia who does not admire the city and sing Toronto's praises. However, when tourists inform Torontonians how wonderful their city is, they tend to think the visitors are blind to reality, lack taste, or are merely being polite. Because they have little sense of urbancentricity, they cannot accept the simple truth: Toronto is a hell of a town. In other cities, they accept the praise readily, confident that it is surely true.

Okay, at this point, you may have realized that I am a Torontonian who is indeed urbancentric. I love the city! Unable to apologize for this failing, I have adjusted to living with the guilt.

Because I love Toronto, I feel comfortable in spoofing its past in the first chapter of the book. However, the other three chapters comprise a serious attempt to chronicle four of the city's downtown neighbourhoods—the villages within.

—An unrepentant Toronto enthusiast

Author's Warning

Many of us learned Canadian history from teachers who were so dry that the Sahara Desert was a wetland in comparison. The various textbooks we stoically thumbed through portrayed our important historical figures as heroes worthy of canonization. However, poems and messages scribbled inside second-hand history texts, on school washroom walls, and backyard fences exposed us to unedited prose and poems about these celebrities of history. These juvenile writers rudely parodied the sacred cows whom our teachers glorified.

- General James Wolfe was an animal.
- Champlain sat on his astrolabe.
- Governor Simcoe was no ruler—he was several inches short.
- The Indians had Etienne Brule for dinner—he was delicious.

The introductory chapter of this book does not attain the lofty heights reached by these young graffiti authors. It is doubtful that it will add to anyone's knowledge of the real history of Toronto and the early-day men and women who built the city. However, the tongue-in-cheek retelling of their exploits may produce a smile, something that our history lessons rarely accomplished.

If readers wish only to explore the history of Toronto in a sensible manner, the author recommends that they do not read the first chapter of the book, but skip to those that follow, as they present a genuine architectural and social study of four of the city's diverse neighbourhoods.

However, skipping the first chapter may deprive readers of some of the most irreverent musings on Toronto's past that have ever disgraced the annals of literature.

Caution

Readers may find the following chapter objectionable.

Reader discretion is advised.

Chapter One:

Toronto's Early Days

**Toronto Harbour in 1793, from an original drawing
found in the possession of Henry Scadding.**

City of Toronto Archives, Fonds 1231, File 1231, Item 896

Those of us who are familiar with the modern metropolis of Toronto, whom its detractors refer to as central Canada's seething cesspool of sin, may find it difficult to envision it in the days before the Europeans arrived, when it was a tranquil landscape. It was a paradise of nothingness. Some people believe that zilch has changed.

However, in the final decade of the eighteenth century, though the site now occupied by the city was an untamed frontier, among the bushes and old-growth forests something was indeed happening. Native hunters, as well as an occasional fur trapper, were nimbly treading through the thick stands of oak, maple, birch, and pine, peering from behind the undergrowth to locate their quarry. As the land was uninhabited, nobody objected to solitary hunters prancing through the woods, peeking out from behind bushes. The French glorified these intrepid trailblazers in their stories and poems, referring to them as "voyageurs."

The linguistically challenged believe that "voyageurs" translates into English as "voyeurs." Alas, this is not true! "Voyeurs" prefer to peek into bedroom and bathroom windows.

Following the American Revolutionary War, the tranquility of the virgin landscape changed drastically when a stampede of Loyalists crashed across the Canadian border to escape the revolting colonies to the south. Although these were the days before the devalued Canadian dollar, the penny-wise Loyalist entrepreneurs knew a good deal when they heard it—the land in Canada was free.

They never mentioned in history books that even if the Loyalists had not revolted against the British Crown, they too could be revolting, as bathtubs, clean undergarments, and deodorants were in short supply.

When the Loyalists arrived in the Canadian wilderness, they were unable to deceive the hunters and trappers already residing in the colony. They knew that nothing in the world was as vicious as a bunch of over-eager bargain hunters. In addition, these wise sharpshooters realized that even though the new immigrants had declared loyalty to King George III, they had not declared their firearms. The competition for game would soon increase. They feared the consequences of gratuitous land grants combined with too many farmers' muskets.

Many people today believe that the "joining together" of gun-toting Loyalists with free land was the origin of the term "shotgun marriages."

*

It is now necessary to provide a little background about the acquisition of the land that became the site of Toronto.

The story begins in 1785, across the briny sea in England. The British government appointed Sir Guy Carlton as governor general of British North America. The following year, they raised him to the peerage as Lord Dorchester, First Baron of Dorchester, in the county of Oxford. Dorchester was quite pleased with his new title. Like most members of the nobility, he knew that it would be an invaluable asset when he arrived in Canada, as colonists were easily impressed with high-sounding titles.

Thus satisfied, he set sail.

Our Lord Dorchester was a real person, not to be confused with hotels and pubs with similar names—the Lord Simcoe, the Lord Elgin, Lord Knows, Lord Forgive Me, and Lord Help Us. We owe Lord Dorchester a great debt of gratitude, as without him, whom would we have named our streets, public squares, cocktail bars, and hotels after?

The tradition of recycling Dorchester's name continued for many years. A few older Torontonians might remember a stripper who appeared in the 1960s at the infamous Victory Theatre on Spadina Avenue. Her stage name was "Dimples Dorchester." Today, I wonder if our portly dear Dorchester possessed a few dimples of his own, but sat on his assets, and never revealed their rippling beauty to the courtesans who hung around the governor's court seeking high-class contacts.

When Dorchester arrived in Canada, the severity of the climate must have shocked him. He likely welcomed the onslaught of a Quebec winter as warmly as the approach of the Bubonic plague. I don't know the French words for "friggin' cold," but even I know what it means when I see my frozen underwear standing upright in the morning, even though I'm not standing in it. I am certain that Dorchester figured it out as well.

I hope that he also discovered that dining on steaming bowls of pea soup provided excellent fortification against the freezing winter winds that funnelled down the St. Lawrence River Valley, and that funnelling copious amount of brandy down his throat added to his defences. The heights of Quebec were not the most important protection against the worst invasion that each year attacked the colony—a Canadian winter.

Compared to the milder climate of the British Isles, Canada was indeed a hostile environment. Lord Dorchester suffered greatly during the dark days of winter, and longed to return to the shores of Mother England. Inside the governor's residence, gazing out the small panes of glass, frosted by the freezing cold, he despaired at the sight of the endless drifts of snow. He likely thought that the gods of "good times" had deserted him. However, eventually, the land warmed and the trees once more displayed hints of greenery.

In the spring of 1787, Dorchester was in an optimistic mood, as his head had cleared of the brandy and his underwear had thawed. He dispatched Deputy Surveyor-General John Collins to the Toronto Carrying Place to negotiate a major real estate deal.

I do not know if John Collins was related to "Tom Collins." I Googled "Tom Collins" but was unable to discover any relationship. However, I found a Web site extolling the virtues of the cocktail referred to as a "Tom's

Collins," a mixture of gin, lemon juice, sugar, and soda water. I concluded that if Tom had existed in the eighteenth century, he would have been too busy at the bar mixing the drink named in his honour to have answered the call of duty from our dear Lord Dorchester.

In 1787, John Collins set forth, and by early July was sailing along the north shore of Lake Ontario in the good ship *Seneca*. Finally, early one morning, Collins arrived in Toronto harbour and ordered the ship's crew to drop anchor. Standing on deck, he must have pondered his dilemma. Dorchester had instructed him to negotiate a major land deal, but there were no real estate companies to be found. Furthermore, they had not yet invented the "Multiple Listing Service," and anyway, if he had heard the term, he would have assumed it merely meant multiple scribbling on latrine walls.

As a result, Collins decided to follow the only course open to him. He opened his own office on the deck of the ship and extended an invitation to three Mississauga Indian chiefs to lunch with him. Mighty Chief Mayor Hazel McCallion of Mississauga fame, though a great leader, was not among them.

Because it was a hot summer afternoon, before discussing the transaction he most likely ordered an alcoholic repast. For obvious reasons, Tom Collins was unavailable, so he probably demanded that a crewmember, perhaps with a name like Daiquiri Dick, deliver the drinks to the deck. Collins had learned from Dorchester that "booze" anaesthetized a person from the heat as well as the cold.

Perhaps this was the origin of Toronto's infamous tradition of the "martini lunch." Without these, the commerce of the city would be paralyzed.

I am confident that Collins poured the alcoholic drinks generously. By the time they reached an agreement, I think they were likely buzzed. How else can we explain that the chiefs consented to sell 250,880 acres for the pitiful sum of seventeen hundred pounds? The huge tract of land extended northward from Lake Ontario and included the site of Toronto as we know it today. It became known as the "Toronto Purchase." It does not surprise me that the land north of Sudbury was not included in the deal. Nobody wanted it.

A few trade goods were included in the deal, and I suspect that among them were several bottles of strong drink. After all, by now everyone knew that his majesty's booze provided excellent insulation against the cold winter months, generating more heat than buckskin underwear.

This story illustrates the point that important negotiations should never be concluded during a martini lunch. However, we should be grateful for Collins' efforts, as it was likely the last time that a government official in Canada purchased anything with taxpayers' funds and received a bargain. Had government consultants been available, they would have caused the price of the land to inflate significantly.

*

In 1791, the British government passed the Constitutional Act, dividing Quebec into two provinces—Lower Canada (modern-day Quebec) and Upper Canada (Ontario). It has been suggested that this started the Ontario-Quebec rivalry, as the French received the ignominious title "Lower," while Ontario was the recipient of the superior designation. Though this theory is not true, in the modern era, some citizens of Quebec still believe that their fellow Canadians in Ontario are "uppity."

Dorchester—the man, not the pub—had not finished his attempts to influence the future of Toronto. He appointed John Graves Simcoe as lieutenant governor of Upper Canada and instructed him to choose a new provincial capital. At the time, it was located at Niagara-on-the-Lake, across the river from the United States and not far from Buffalo. Simcoe agreed that it was wise to choose a more secure location.

Today, those who disagree with the governor's decision to relocate should remember that Mrs. Simcoe was fourteen years her husband's junior. Surely, we can sympathize with a man who had a young wife within close proximity to Buffalo. Thankfully, credit cards and shopping malls did not exist at the time. However, it was better to play it safe.

After serious deliberation, I suspect as long as three or four minutes, he chose Toronto as his new capital, even though it had no virtues except that it possessed an excellent harbour and was not close to the American border. Today, many Canadians remain convinced that Toronto still lacks any virtues, and that there is still nothing of note in Toronto, except the bank "notes" in the hated financial institutions of Bay Street.

There were other reasons why Simcoe was anxious to depart from Niagara-on-the-Lake. Try to imagine the town in the 1790s. There was no Shaw Festival, and the town lacked savoir faire. There were no wineries or winery restaurants. No wonder Mrs. Simcoe accepted her husband's decision to depart from the small town. Besides, she likely wanted to dwell in a place with bright lights, like those found on Yonge Street today.

Simcoe sailed from Niagara-on-the-Lake and arrived at the Toronto Carrying Place in the early hours of July 30, 1793. He moored the HMS *Mississauga* at the mouth of the Humber River and awaited daylight to venture ashore. When he stepped on deck at day's first light, the scenery that greeted him contained nothing but trees—trees—and more trees.

It was a virgin landscape.

Today, some critics feel that this was the last time anyone employed the word "virgin" to refer to anything in Toronto. Considering the city's propensity toward the prim and proper, this is a very strange accusation.

On this sunny day in August 1793, to say that Simcoe was "up the stump" would have been an understatement. The royal suite at the King Eddie was obviously not available, and so he was forced to pitch his canvas tents beside the lake.

To make matters worse, the tents were second hand, Simcoe having purchased them at an auction in London. At one time, they had been owned by Captain James Cook of "South Pacific" fame. Contrary to common belief, James Cook had nothing to do with the Rodgers and Hammerstein musical of that name. He merely explored the Pacific Ocean for the British government and discovered the Sandwich Islands.

It is a pernicious rumour that Cook later authored the "Sandwich Section" of the *Michelin Guide*, and named the "two-faced open sandwiches" in honour of British politicians. Though he may have considered them five-star men, he knew that were crusty and their edicts were difficult to swallow.

In the encampment beside the lake, we doubt that Mrs. Simcoe teased her husband about his choice of pre-owned tents. However, we cannot help but wonder if behind the governor's back, the troops were quietly crooning the words of the song "Second-Hand Rose."

If Simcoe ever became aware of such disrespectful behaviour, he would have firmly put a stop to it, fearing that the men might eventually begin referring to him as "Rosie." It is fun to speculate what might have happened if he had received such a humorous nickname. Would he have received offers to perform on the stages of gay nightclubs or "women's only" strip joints? Such entreaties would hardly have been dignified proposals to suggest to a representative of the Crown. Fortunately, the point was moot, as the settlement lacked even a tavern, never mind a nightclub.

Within a day or two of their arrival, Mrs. Simcoe toured the small settlement huddled along the shoreline. The first evening, she undoubtedly discovered that the candles in the windows of the few log cabins at Toronto hardly qualified it as a place of "bright lights." In addition, today, we know that some of the colonial officials were not exactly bright lights either. It wasn't just the floorboards of the homes in Toronto that were "plank-thick."

*

In Simcoe's encampment beside Lake Ontario, there was plenty of open space, but as far as we know, no open bar. This was a pity, as the area was so heavily loaded with trees and bushes that imbibing until one was similarly loaded was an excellent way to immunize oneself against the many insects that inhabited the forest.

In addition, we suspect that the guest towels in Simcoe's camp were of poor quality, because there were no reports of anyone stealing them. This illustrates the pitiful state of the governor's hostelry. In addition, it reveals that even colonial-era thieving sycophants had standards.

It has been recorded that the Simcoes dined on the foods and game that were available from "forest, lake, and stream." Given this description, it is possible to speculate on the meals that they served. I am confident that not everyone appreciated the "filet of raccoon," "skunk Wellington," and "carp bisque." Intense arguments were certain to have occurred when deciding the proper wines to serve. This was an important consideration, because a plenteous supply of strong drink was a necessity when consuming the severe frontier diet. The true wine connoisseurs in Simcoe's entourage likely insisted that the fruity bouquet of a Burgundy clashed with the delicate aroma of the skunk Wellington and suggested that a light-bodied claret was preferable.

I think that the debate ended when they discovered that the only liquid available was water from the lake. To make matters worse, Toronto's harbour water during the 1790s was not as "full bodied" as it is today. Dumping garbage into it for over two hundred years has increased its viscosity.

Future provincial politicians took note of the difficulties Simcoe experienced and invented government expense accounts. These permitted officials to avoid arguments concerning wining and dining, as the bills remained secret, allowing great creativity when determining the amounts to be reimbursed. Today, however, there are those who think that the foul odour from the abuse of public funds exceeds that which was emitted by the skunk meat of yesteryear.

Apart from the difficulties of the dining table, Simcoe had another problem that bothered him. He thought that the name Toronto sounded "outlandishly foreign." I think that he preferred good old English names, such as Yorkshire pudding. Even if he did, he was unable to name the town after a pudding. Fortunately, the youngest son of George III, the Duke of York, provided a solution. He had recently been victorious over the French in Holland. On August 24, 1793, Simcoe changed the name of the tiny settlement from Toronto to York.

Today, I cannot help but wonder if the name York was an abbreviation of Yorkshire pudding.

The Land before Settlement

The earliest descriptions of Toronto are contained in the writings of Mrs. Simcoe. She explored the forests surrounding the encampment, often walking for miles. She reported that the land was richly covered with deciduous trees, including many stands of oak, maple, pine, and butternut. Beneath the canopy, there was much undergrowth and an abundance of gooseberries. In her diary she wrote: "When stewed, [they] were found to be excellent."

She did not mention that they were also excellent when fermented to produce wine and cordials, so we are left to surmise what became of the leftover fruit. *If* she engaged in the sinful activity of winemaking—and if *The Sound of Music* had been written—we can imagine her bottling her home brew, crooning the words of the song "These Are a Few of My Favourite Things." I am just speculating, but I bet her voice would have soared to operatic heights in belting forth: *The hills are alive with the sound of music. I've booze that'll last for a thousand years ...!*

I know this never happened, but I enjoy sober speculation.

However, her written descriptions of the countryside do indicate that she was "high" on something. She wrote that the luscious meadows were flooded with summer sunshine, where millions of yellow and black butterflies darted and fluttered amid the bushes and delicate flowers. Wild ducks flew overhead, she said, and above the clear water of the harbour circled thousands of enchanting gulls.

She considered these aggressive birds enchanting? The anaesthetic effects of gooseberry wine can be amazing. However, in truth, the forests surrounding York were amazingly delightful. There was an extreme beauty to the severity of the wilderness and the unspoiled forests. The land was ripe for government development. Why leave a good thing alone?

It was not long before the Queen's Rangers left the encampment beside the lake and commenced clearing the forests. They viewed trees as obstacles to civilization and felt that they should chop them down as soon as possible. Elizabeth Simcoe reported that the sound of crashing trees was constant from early morning until sundown.

Today, I wonder if the sounds emitted by the "crashing bores" around the dinner table were equally as noisy. Conversation was bound to be uninspired in an era without CTV, the CBC, reality shows, and endless reruns of *Little Mosque on the Prairie*.

In addition, Elizabeth Simcoe wrote that each day the cutting of trees was so abundant that the air was pungent with the smell of new wood. She never mentioned if another scent permeated the air. Remember, the encampment lacked showers.

Eventually surveyors arrived to measure and stake out building lots. In an attempt to lure the prosperous elite from Niagara-on-the-Lake, Governor Simcoe provided generous land grants to a few of his privileged friends. This established the tradition in Ontario of the government granting financial rewards to political confidants. In Ottawa, in later years, the tradition became known as an appointment to the senate.

*

The town of York, as laid out by Governor Simcoe in 1793, consisted of ten square blocks at the eastern end of the small harbour. Clearing the land to create building lots and streets was not an easy task. The area was covered by old-growth forest, some of the trees having existed for centuries, the likes of which would never be seen again. Many of the pines were three or four feet in diameter, with the oaks and maples often larger. Chopping down the forest was arduous, and removing the stumps was laborious.

Because of these endeavours, a basic principle became firmly entrenched in the psyche of Toronto—chop down anything that is old, well built, and attractive. It can always be replaced by faceless glass and steel.

At the beginning of the nineteenth century, the houses of York were huddled close to the shores of the lake in a confined area at the eastern end of the harbour. During those early years, York likely appeared somewhat similar to the Niagara-on-the-Lake of today, but far less tidy and certainly without the hordes of summer tourists. I should also point out that there were no ice cream parlours or statues of George Bernard Shaw on the main street of York. However, there was a plentiful supply of garbage and "well-fed rats." For information on the latter, Google "government consultants and lobbyists."

The houses of York were located on a grid pattern, set back from the lot lines, with gardens and orchards surrounding them. Unfortunately, unlike the Niagara area, the climate was not suitable for viniculture. However, living in close proximity to one's neighbours allowed another type of grapevine to flourish—the gossip grapevine.

None of the gossip of York has survived into modern times. However, judging by the comments whispered over the back fences of today and those texted on cell phones, the snippets of tittle-tattle in the nineteenth century were likely as ripe as the garbage in the trenches surrounding their houses.

However, the colonists enjoyed an advantage over the gossipers of today. When bored with tongue-lashing a neighbourhood, they could enjoy a public hanging or the brutal lashing of a criminal. Despite having no *Hockey Night in Canada* to watch on television, life in the old days had its entertaining moments.

Years later, the area surrounding Niagara-on-the-Lake became profuse with wineries and home to the second largest permanent theatre company in North America. The blend of wine and theatre has proved quite fortuitous. Those who fail to enjoy the performances on stage can imbibe fermented juice until they could care less. A bottle or two of wine is able to transform any musical at the Royal George Theatre into an operatic masterpiece. Personally, I believe that George Bernard Shaw would have approved of the union of good theatre with vintage wines. This was no "shotgun marriage."

The Shakespearean Festival in the city of Stratford did not have this advantage, but it has become the largest permanent theatre company in North America. It is a magnet for those who enjoy excellent summer theatre. For several decades, the "thrust stage" at the Festival Theatre has captured the imagination of theatregoers. The critics who review the plays at Stratford tend to be more insightful, as they are usually sober, as even Pelee Island wines are too far away to be imbibed.

*

Shortly after Governor Simcoe relocated the provincial government from the Niagara Region and established it at York, he ordered the military to construct fortifications near the western entrance to the harbour. No doubt, few of the colonists greeted the idea with enthusiasm, as they preferred Dorchester's method of "bottle fortification." However, once the construction began, I am certain that they admitted that it was a novel idea, and although it was hard on the back, it was easier on the liver. This was fortunate, as Dodd's Little Liver Pills had not yet been invented.

When Fort York was completed, they referred to the land surrounding it as the Military Reserve. It extended west to present-day Dufferin Street, east to Spadina, north to Queen Street, and south to Lake Ontario.

In the 1790s, the Toronto Islands of modern times was a peninsula, as there was no eastern gap. A severe storm severed the connection to the mainland in 1858. When it was a peninsula, it provided shelter against the storms of the lake and offered protection should American forces invade from across Lake Ontario. People from the town of York could walk to the islands. It's a pity the islands did not remain as a peninsula, as it would have reduced crowding at today's ferry terminals. In addition, people who wish to fly from the island airport could have walked to the terminal from Ward's Island.

It would serve them right.

I suppose Elizabeth missed the bright lights of her native isle, because the Simcoes finally decided to return to England. During the years following the departure of the Simcoes, York continued to expand. An increase in population was inevitable in a town with no television or Internet services to amuse the inhabitants.

*

Few people today realize how extreme the deprivations at York were—no one owned a cell phone, and the only cable companies were those that manufactured the cables for public hangings.

However, during the next few years, York attracted settlers, many of whom were hired by the government. These "bright lights" knew about expense accounts, but the rip-off known as "severance packages" had not yet been invented. Research has proven that this was not entirely true, as astute politicians had known about them for several years, as evidenced by the fact that during the French Revolution, Louis XVI of France received a severance package at the conclusion of his reign.

Not all immigrants at York were employed by the government. Some commenced commercial enterprises or worked in the many trades and leisure activities required by the growing population.

Simcoe named Yonge Street after the British secretary of war, who, despite his name, in due course became an elderly man. They eventually extended the street as far as the shores of Lake Simcoe, and in the years ahead, to Cochrane,

Ontario. Today, it is reputed to be the longest street in the world. Some detractors declare that it is a road "from nowhere to nowhere."

In addition to Yonge Street, a military supply road was built. It became the Dundas Street of today. It was named after a friend of Governor Simcoe, Henry Dundas, First Viscount of Melville.

To the east of the town, they constructed a small wooden bridge to span the Don River, at the foot of the hill at Winchester Street, allowing the town to spread eastward. Today, residents who dwell to the east of the Don Valley still complain about the things that "spread" from the downtown core. I do not know what the word "spread" implies, but I suspect it includes "verbal manure" from City Hall.

They erected York's first wooden frame house at the corner of King and Sherbourne streets. The settlers who dwelt in crude log cabins along the shoreline envied the edifice. Perhaps I am wrong, but I believe that today, psychiatrists refer to those who are jealous of other people's building erections as suffering from "erection envy." Though the laws of Moses do not mention "erection envy," they clearly state that "coveting your neighbour's wife" is verboten. I believe it applies even if she is bending over in the garden at the time.

*

Now let us return to the erections of York, where apart from one house, few people envied anything that had been built.

However, things were changing.

The town finally extended a wharf into the harbour, at the foot of Bathurst Street, to facilitate the loading and unloading of ships. While men laboured building the wharf, others toiled under the summer sun to erect the colony's first parliament buildings on Parliament Street, near Palace Street, which is today Berkeley Street. The confusion engendered by the street names was directly proportional to the confusion experienced by the legislators, who when in session, passed many baffling laws.

Though I cannot prove it, I suspect that beneath the light of the moon, some men at York laboured unloading illegal rum and brandy from ships anchored in secluded harbours on the outskirts of town. This was likely the beginning of one of Toronto's main commercial enterprises of today—an importer of sin.

In addition, during the early-days of York, there was a brisk trade in animal skins. Perhaps this accounts for today's activities in certain bars and on a number of street corners in the wee hours of the morning, where there is still a brisk trade selling skin for cash.

Today, those who purchase "skin" with credit cards, and thus collect air miles, extend the value of their dubious transactions. If a person pays cash, similar to the days of old, they avoid paying government taxes. Perhaps GST means **G**ratis for **S**ex **T**rade.

In 1798, a school was founded by William Cooper, although it was a private educational facility and attended only by the children of wealthy families.

Meanwhile, on Frederick Street, south of King Street, East Mile's Hotel opened to supply visitors with accommodations. Its beverage room provided relief to thirsty men on a balmy summer day and alcoholic warmth on a frosty winter evening. Dorchester's discoveries were still honoured in the pubs of York. After a mug or two (or six) of grog, the town looked so attractive that it inspired many a flowery letter to be mailed home to Mother Britain. As a result, the following year, York's first post office was established.

In 1800, the town's first well was dug, which meant the residents of York no longer depended on the streams or the lake for their supply of water. I have it on good authority that the new source of liquid refreshment did nothing to decrease the amount of spirits consumed.

By 1801, shipping in the harbour had increased and it was necessary to appoint a collector of customs. William Allen was appointed to the position. He accumulated sufficient funds to become a rich man, enabling him to donate land to the city that today is an idyllic green space at Jarvis and Carlton Streets—Allan Gardens. Today, panhandlers in the park continue to solicit money to honour the fine old tradition that Mr. Allen began in 1801.

In 1803, land was designated for the construction of an Anglican church on King Street East, and the parish of St. James was born. Finally, there was a place on Sunday morning to atone for the sins of indulgence on the previous Saturday night. In any era, sleeping through a sermon is always a good way to recover from the sin of immoderation.

The same year, Governor Hunter set aside land for a public market, naming it after the patron saint of Canada—St. Lawrence. Today, many Canadians consider the most important saints to be St. Timothy of Horton, St. Harvey's, and St. Swiss Chalet. Small fragments from the robe of St. Timothy of Horton are considered sacred and are known as "Timbits."

More shops appeared along King Street, as it attracted the most carriages and foot traffic. In 1805, Samuel Jackson opened Toronto's first haberdashery. Those who were unable to pronounce the word "haberdashery" went to a clothing shop instead. The same year, the city ordered its first official census, along with other statistical data. It was discovered that the death rate in York was "one per person."

The same year, a brewery and apothecary opened. Fortunately, they founded both establishments the same year. Farmers who came to town and overindulged now had somewhere to purchase a remedy for their swollen heads.

In colonial days, very little entertainment was available. One of the favourite evening pastimes was to attend dances and dinners in the officers' mess at Fort York. Some thought that they referred to the dining room as the "mess," due to the many officers who showed their disdain when offered skunk pie by tossing it on the floor.

Untrue!

For the politically well connected at York, the governor's residence at the fort, located a short distance to the west of the fort, was the centre of social life. Francis Gore was appointed the new lieutenant governor in 1806 and officially took office on August 25 of that year. In mid-September, the new governor opened the autumn social season with an evening of dancing and dining. During the months ahead, the winter's entertainment activities appeared in rapid succession.

I am hesitant to mention the following rumour, but it's too juicy to ignore. It was said that one of the most popular ways to avoid the freezing cold was to hop in and out of each other's bed. Some sources refer to this as "burlap hopping," and state that it was the origin of the phrase "a hop in the sack."

I've even heard that the most common phrase whispered at parties was "Shall we hit the sack to partake of a little heat?"

Whether or not this information was accurate, it is true that before long the population of little York greatly expanded.

On frosty evenings, to attend a dance at the governor's residence, women and their escorts in their horse-drawn sleighs travelled westward from the town of York to the fort beside Garrison Creek. The trek was often a lively cavalcade, with merchants and men of distinction shouting and laughing as they rode through the winter landscape. The women chatted amiably as they journeyed in their sleighs through the trails in the woods, huddled beneath thick blankets. I suspect that some sipped a wee bit of whiskey. After all, "blankets and booze" were the mainstays of colonial life.

After traversing the woods, one could see twinkling pinpoints of light from the fort in the distance, sparkling invitingly through the darkness. On reaching Fort York, guests entered the garrison by the timbered eastern gateway. The sentries saluted as they silently observed the visitors, the tinkle of harness bells and the sound of excited voices filling the air as they entered the interior of the fort. Passing through the garrison grounds, they exited at the western gate, then, crossed the small bridge spanning Garrison Creek. On the western side of the stream was Government House. As they arrived, the visitors were able to hear music floating on the crisp, night air.

Today, the entertainment district honours this fine old tradition. In the early-morning hours, shrieking 905-ers and young condo-dwellers fill the air with boisterous shouting, along with the sweet bouquet of funny grass. It is heart warming to know that they maintain the cherished rituals of yesteryear with such ardent fervour.

God bless our historic-minded younger generation.

By European standards, Government House was a rough dwelling of no architectural importance, constructed of rough-hewn timbers and only one storey in height. Someone once wrote that it resembled an over-sized privy. However, to the citizens of York, it was an immensely significant part of their lives.

The governor's abode contained multi-paned windows overlooking the parade ground, located between the fort and the residence. On nights when the governor entertained, the lights from the windows glowed in the darkness and spilled outward, reflecting across the snow. The revellers within, dancing beside the enormous crackling fireplace, were protected from the severity of the winter night.

They were boisterous affairs. Because of the prodigious quaffing of ale and acres of unspoiled snow, some historians claim that it was on one of these occasions that some of the men invented a certain well-known method of writing in the snow. Research has proven this untrue, as winters at York were too cold for a man to expose his "quill."

The personal secretary of Lieutenant-Governor Gore was Major William Halton. His position was one of considerable importance in the colony. He signed many of the legal documents in the name of the governor and officiated at major functions. Most of the consequential events in the daily life of pioneer York came under his scrutiny.

In April 1807, William Halton placed his signature, on behalf of Governor Gore, to the decree that appointed Mr. Stuart as the teacher of the "District School in York and the Home Districts." Such well-known personalities as John Ridout, William Hamilton, Allan McNabb, the Jarvis sisters, and George Boulton Junior attended this institute of learning. Because of their family connections, as adults, these children became very prominent citizens of the colony. People eventually referred to them as the "family compact." I will mention this group again later in the narrative.

William Halton guided the reins of the royal coach when Governor and Mrs. Annabella Gore travelled from the garrison at Fort York to the town of York to attend the Parliament of Upper Canada. In those days, the trip from the town to Fort York was considered a significant distance to travel. The western limit of the town was Peter Street, and between it and the fort were fields and forests. To the west, beyond the fort, there was only wilderness. The Parliament building was located at the eastern end of the town, near the Don River.

One morning in 1807, Calvin Banister unbolted the doors of the city's first saddle shop. The same year, Reverend Stewart created a public school to educate the children of the poor, although few attended, as most children of school age remained at home to assist with the myriad household chores demanded in an age without advanced technology. Others were employed outside the homes as child labourers.

They opened a library in 1810. In 1811, the site of today's condominium at 50 Camden Street was Crown land, but in this year, the governor bestowed it as a royal land grant to William Halton.

The War of 1812

As tension between Great Britain and the United States increased, it was feared that open conflict was pending between Canada and her neighbour to the south. It was far more serious than the perennial argument over whether tea or coffee should be served for breakfast, or if a nation's head of state should be a president or a king.

In July of the previous year, Major-General Isaac Brock had arrived at York, taking command of the military affairs of the province. He reinforced the fortifications of Fort York, and it is rumoured that he established a pub for the troops. This is this untrue. Perhaps historians misunderstood the meaning of the term "high-spirited troops."

When Governor Gore returned to England in October of 1811, Isaac Brock became both the civil and military commander, with the title of "President and Administrator," a rather "republican" title for the chief executive of a royal colony. We do not know if the troops sang "Hail to the Chief" to him when he entered the fort.

The same year Brock entered Upper Canada, a young lieutenant also arrived—James Fitzgibbon. In Europe, both he and Brock had fought in the Napoleonic Wars. Fitzgibbon was one of Brock's favourite officers, having secured for him several promotions without the usual payment of funds. The residents of York did not consider this unusual. Simcoe had already established the principle of giving "privileges to the privileged." Brock encouraged Fitzgibbon to pursue private studies to improve his education. Early in the year 1812, Fitzgibbon resigned his army commission to study full time, in hopes of eventually earning further promotions. A few of the more advanced government positions required that a man be intelligently educated.

I believe that in the modern era, this stipulation has been abolished for elected positions in government.

Arriving in Canada with the Forty-ninth Regiment, Brock was an officer of considerable military experience. He commanded much attention, with his striking features, blond hair, and blue eyes. He was over six feet in height, which was unusually tall for these years. In addition to his handsome appearance, he possessed gracious manners, impressing those whom he encountered.

Brock was also immensely popular with the troops, as he did not permit the officers to drill the men for long durations during freezing temperatures and insisted that they be properly clothed and fed. Under his leadership, morale rose and desertion from the ranks ceased. Besides, as they were in the middle of the wilderness, there was nowhere for the men to go.

At the social evenings at Government House, located on the west side of Fort York, the women always eagerly anticipated the commander's presence. On such occasions, he was attired in the ornate scarlet tunic of a British officer. He wore a white sash around his waist, and a polished silver sword hung from his belt. He was long remembered by those whom he met. Star-struck women said that he was such an excellent horseman that he looked like part of the horse. I am certain that more than a few envious husbands agreed, muttering, "He looks like the horse's rear end."

*

On June 18, 1812, war with the United States commenced. Unlike today, York's business community did not welcome a summer invasion of Americans charging across the border. After several victories on the battlefield, General Brock was killed at the Battle of Queenston Heights. The news of his death struck the fragile community of York like a thunderbolt. Many feared the war would be lost without his leadership.

In April of 1813, the Americans sailed across Lake Ontario and attacked York. When it was obvious that the struggle to secure the fort was doomed, the British lit a fuse to the powder magazine and swiftly retreated. When the powder detonated, it rained shrapnel for a radius of over a mile. Very little of Fort York survived. During the years ahead, debris from the explosion was found in the fields and embedded in the trees. It is possible that the older trees of the St. Andrew's Playground of today were among them, as photographs taken around 1910 reveal that they were already mature trees at that time.

When the American invaders entered the town, they set fire to the parliament buildings and carried away the parliamentary symbol of authority, the "mace." In addition, while in the building, they discovered the ceremonial wig of the speaker of the house, and mistakenly thought it was a human scalp. When the troops returned home, they claimed that the British were "scalpers."

Today, I glow with pride when I see the descendents of these "scalpers" outside the Air Canada Centre, particularly when the Leafs play against the Habs. I have even seen them around the opera house and Roy Thomson Hall. Some unkind souls say that Torontonians will scalp their grandmothers if the price is right. We do indeed honour our traditions.

In addition, today, some state that the infamous wig from the War of 1812 eventually surfaced on the head of Mel Lastman, who wore it honourably and ignored the surreptitious smiles, claiming it was a hair weave. I am certain they are wrong.

In 1934, in honour of the city's centennial, the mace was returned to Toronto and today is on display at Fort York. No one knows the real location of the speaker's wig.

*

One of the best-remembered stories of the War of 1812 was the exploits of Laura Secord, who, contrary to rumours, was not Canada's first chocolate maker. She "sallied forth" through the "enemy-infested woods" of the Niagara area. Have you ever noticed that in most heroic tales, the heroes "sally forth" in the "dead of night" and invariably choose "enemy-infested environs"? Such wording is a prerequisite for these stories.

Be it as it may, Laura's deeds were impressive.

Late one evening, little Laura overheard a few American troops discussing plans to attack the British near the town of Beaver Dams on the following day. She knew that Lieutenant James Fitzgibbon was on a military stake out, so she sallied forth in the dead of night through the enemy-infested woods, employing a cow as a decoy. Thinking she was a mere farmer's wife, the American sentries allowed her to pass through their lines. As a result, Laura was successful in warning Fitzgibbon of the impending attack.

In retelling the events of that portentous night, some misguided soul thought that Laura had confused a "stake-out" with a "steak-out," and that was why she brought along the cow.

Due to her information, Fitzgibbon successfully captured 450 enemy infantrymen, 50 cavalrymen, 2 field guns, and a partridge in a pear tree. These figures are accurate, although the "partridge in a pear tree" is my own addition. It seemed to be a natural conclusion to the sentence. However, it's true that he accomplished his victory by bluffing the enemy into surrendering by offering to prevent the Indians from attacking. The Americans were unaware that Fitzgibbon commanded just forty-eight soldiers and a band of only four hundred Indians. The enemy force had been superior in both numbers and artillery.

Fitzgibbon was highly praised for his quick-witted actions.

However, according to some rather dubious sources, because of his ability to bluff, in the years ahead nobody would play poker with him. Some say that to compensate for this sleight, they bestowed on him the official title of "York's First Bluffer" and named the Scarborough Bluffs after him.

This is all historic bumf.

*

Following the war with the United States, on September 29, 1815, Lieutenant-Governor Gore returned to York and resumed his role as governor. He was a wise governor, wise enough not to hang around the colony during a dangerous war.

Governor Gore again appointed William Halton as his secretary, but he served for only one year. Halton returned to Britain in 1816, in his pocket the deed for the land where the condominium 50 Camden site is today located.

This same year, James Fitzgibbon assumed the role of adjutant-general of militia for Upper Canada. Now in England, William Halton sold the Camden site to James Fitzgibbon, the transaction arranged through his lawyer in Upper Canada, Duncan Cameron. They registered the title to the land on March 8, 1817. The price paid was 270 pounds. Throughout the next few years, Fitzgibbon was involved in various financial endeavours, using his Camden property as collateral.

Governor Gore departed from the colony for the final time in June of 1817 and returned to England. Perhaps he too had grown tired of the dim-bulb colonists at York, and like Elizabeth Simcoe, yearned for the bright lights of London.

However, some unkind courtiers who considered themselves witty, said that when Gore arrived home and encountered the most recent hangers-on at the royal court, he realized that a few of them were missing a few volts and that the court of the king had too many queens. To paraphrase the words of the Canadian humorist Stephen Leacock, such courtiers should drop dead, dig a hole, and bury themselves.

James Fitzgibbon, the hero of the War of 1812 and the owner of the Camden property, was now a well-known figure in the town of York. Henry Scadding, in his book *Toronto of Old*, referred to Fitzgibbon as one of "the reverend seniors, who assembled habitually in the church at York." This was the old wooden church of St. James, at King and Church Streets, not the structure of today. In addition, Scadding, in his book, wrote the following about Fitzgibbon:

> His tall, muscular figure, ever in buoyant motion; his grey good-humoured, vivacious eye beaming out from underneath a bushy, light-coloured eyebrow; the cheery ring of his voice and its animated utterances were familiar to everyone.
>
> In the midst of a gathering of the young, whether in the schoolroom or the playground, his presence was always warmly hailed. They at once recognized him as a sympathizer with themselves, in their ways and

wants, and had ever ready for them words of hope and encouragement.

(*Toronto of Old,* Henry Scadding, Oxford University Press, Toronto, 1966)

Other sources state that Fitzgibbon was a person of military bearing and exceptional strength, possessing both courage and wit. Had he survived into the modern era, he would have been a great candidate for mayor of Toronto. However, we have no idea if he had a broom of sufficient size to sweep away the wasteful financial practices at City Hall. In the nineteenth century, a man's "broom size" was never discussed in polite company.

In 1817, a police force was created. Without these brave men, there would never have been any TV shows, such as *Blue Murder, Flashpoint, Law and Order,* and *CSI.* The boys in blue are not to be confused with "bar-boys of the night," although they too work nightshifts.

The first brick house was built in 1818, and in 1819, the first bank was incorporated. Building homes necessitated mortgages, so it was fortuitous that a bank was created so quickly. Today, banks and developers remain bosom pals, exchanging tit for tat over martini lunches.

In 1820, the town's first theatrical stage came to life. On the inaugural occasion, I understand that the famous Irish singer, Mary O'Lanza, charmed the audience. This was likely only a rumour.

Two years later, the first Presbyterian Church commenced services, this being important, as there was now a church congregation to condemn the dubious "carrying-on" in the theatre.

**Toronto Harbour in 1820, from an original drawing by Sir
Peregrine Maitland, Lieut. Governor of Upper Canada.**

City of Toronto Archives, Fonds 1231, Item 895

In 1825, a dental practice was begun. Politicians could now have their decayed teeth pulled. This shortened political debates, as getting one's gums into an issue never provided much argumentative pull.

In 1826, James Fitzgibbon became involved in another historic event in the town of York. He begrudgingly collected the funds that a court had awarded to William Lyon Mackenzie. The money was compensation for his printing press, which had been thrown into the lake by a group of young Tory hotheads. As Fitzgibbon had openly sided with the Tories, the affair did not endear him to Mackenzie.

In 1827, Fitzgibbon secured the position of clerk of the Canadian House of Assembly. Mackenzie viewed the appointment as a sinecure position that was undeserving. In his newspaper, he severely criticized Fitzgibbon.

**York (Toronto) Harbour in 1830, with the
fish market in the foreground.**

City of Toronto Archives, Fonds 1231, Item 96

In 1832, a riot broke out in the town, a feud involving a struggle between the Reformers, led by Mackenzie, and the Tories, who sided with the Family Compact. Fitzgibbon intervened in the fight on the street in front of Mackenzie's printing shop. Not to be outdone, Mackenzie dared Fitzgibbon to call out the troops. Fitzgibbon threatened to arrest Mackenzie and charge him in court with being the instigator of the riot. Mackenzie backed down, and Fitzgibbon escorted him to his home, shoving him inside the front door. It was a colourful and action-packed scene. Mackenzie retreated to wait for a more opportune moment, while Fitzgibbon basked in the sunlight of adoration from his powerful friends, and, for all we know, consumed a drop or two of moonshine.

*

In this decade, on Terauley Street (near Queen and Bay Streets), there were large pools of stagnant water, where rotting vegetable matter and decomposing garbage had been thrown. The air was contaminated with noxious and poisonous inhalations. The site eventually became the location of the second City Hall of Toronto, now referred to as Old City Hall.

There was no connection between noxious gasses and the location of the City Hall.

In 1832, a board of health for the town of York was created, and Fitzgibbon was placed in charge. His appointment was in response to the Terauley Street situation, where outbreaks of cholera continued to occur. The disease was spread by contaminated water, and as bacterium were unknown, there was no effective medical treatment available. In 1832, before the plague ended, 273 persons died. It was the responsibility of the new board of health to arrange for the collection of garbage and maintain the sewers. This eased the situation, but each year the deaths from cholera did not fully cease until one late autumn, when a killing frost descended over the town.

Despite the regard in which Fitzgibbon was held by the residents of York, and the importance of his official positions, he received much prestige but little monetary reward. He resented this oversight and, as a result, failed to take seriously the duties involved with his various appointments. Often he did not attend the required meetings. He likely thought he was an Ottawa senator, even though he was unable to skate.

Mackenzie wrote in his newspaper about the evils of the patronage system in Upper Canada and selected Fitzgibbon as a prime target. It was only a matter of time before blood was spilt, a situation far more serious than tipping over your neighbour's backhouse.

*

Discontent continued to ferment. York was a hotbed of unrest, much of it emanating from the reformers, who were constantly agitating for change. The wealthy families, referred to as the Family Compact, possessed great privilege and authority. Many people deeply resented this concentration of power, especially the farmers.

Meanwhile, the influential families of York believed that they too had received the "short shift." Similar to modern CEOs, who believe that their salaries, company perks, and expense accounts do not adequately compensate them for their long hours of relentless toil on the golf courses, the members of the Family Compact resented the demands of the reformers. The chances of turmoil being avoided were becoming as dim as the governor and his executive council. They were unaware that something was fermenting. However, in fairness, all colonials fermented something or other.

However, on the surface, daily life at York continued. In 1833, a horse boat in the harbour provided ferry service across the bay to the Spit (Toronto Islands). In the same year, the land to the west of the city was steadily being cleared of trees.

In 1834, there were seven newspapers in York, servicing a population of 9,252. There was a great deal of daily news to be reported, as York was the provincial capital. Mackenzie's was one of the influential periodicals, and his editorials in the *Colonial Advocate* helped fan the flames of discontent. The year 1834 was important, as the town was incorporated as a city, with William Lyon Mackenzie as its first mayor. The "Firebrand" had finally been elected to power. The name of the new city was to be Toronto. Citizens approved of the name change, as they resented people referring to their town as "Little York," to distinguish it from New York City. The name Toronto was an Indian word, meaning, "carry place."

City council annexed the land between Peter Street and Fort York, which remained mostly forested. The western boundary of the city was Peter Street. One of the first acts of the fledging administration was to order that the forest to the west of Spadina be cleared of trees. Mackenzie failed to realize that without trees, troops would be able to see the rebels more easily, and line their britches with musket balls.

However, it should be pointed out that having burning musket balls in one's underwear was not the origin of the term "hot pants."

The Rebellion of 1837

On the death of King William IV in 1837, Victoria ascended the throne of England to much celebration throughout the land. The Duke of Wellington, the hero of Waterloo, who remained a frequent visitor at the Royal Court, joined in the festivities. However, 1837 was not destined to remain a year in which Her Majesty was to be "amused" for long. Across the sea in Upper Canada, the struggle was intensifying between the Family Compact and the reformers. The Rebellion of 1837 was to tarnish the glory of the first year of the young queen's reign.

The mood of Toronto became ominous in the autumn of 1837, with opinions hardening on both sides. Discontent eventually exploded into open conflict, which once more thrust Fitzgibbon on the central stage of Upper Canada. In some respects, the drama of the rebellion was more of a musical comedy than an opera. There was no fat lady, no chorus crooning in the background, and no big-bosomed women strutting past the scenery.

Fitzgibbon knew nothing about opera, but he was fully aware of the troubling situation, and was one of the few prepared to take action. Having experienced firsthand the explosive personality of Mackenzie, he warned Sir Francis Bond Head (often referred to by the colonists as Bone Head) of the impending danger. Some of the executive council accused Fitzgibbon of being an alarmist and over-anxious for conflict.

Bond Head listened to his ill-informed advisors and sent most of the troops to Lower Canada to help crush the rebellion in that province. Even in those days, the needs of Quebec took precedence in Canadian politics. However, as a precaution, Bond Head appointed Fitzgibbon as adjutant-general of the militia.

The evening following his appointment, Fitzgibbon sent a group of militiamen north of the city. They situated themselves behind a fence on Yonge Street, near where Carlton Street is located today. In the darkness, the troops, under the command of Sheriff William Jarvis, confronted a band of rebels marching south to Toronto to join with other sympathizers. A few shots were fired, and in the ensuing confusion, both sides became afraid for their lives and fled.

It is a pity that Maple Leaf Gardens had not been built. The combatants could have entered the arena and settled the fight with hockey sticks. In a civilized manner, they could have checked each other into the boards and cracked a few heads. If the skirmish had ended in this manner, the Leafs of today might have inherited some of that fighting tradition.

The next clash occurred on a cold December day. Fitzgibbon led the loyalist troops up Yonge Street, a short distance to the north of the Eglinton Avenue of today, to Montgomery's Tavern, to disperse the rebels. The revolting farmers fled. Besides, I understand that the supply of ale had run out, so there was no reason to stay. This effectively ended the rebellion, and greatly enhanced Fitzgibbon's reputation.

In 1838, Fitzgibbon served as judge advocate during the trials that followed the insurrection. Some hard-hearted souls say that hanging usurpers by the neck is more satisfying than shooting them. This is because hangings last longer, allowing a person sufficient time to knit while heads roll. For further information, Google "Madame Defarge."

I do not know if Fitzgibbon enjoyed the hangings, but the trials of the rebels were the highlight of his career. If he had been Madame Lafarge, by the time the executions ended, he would have likely completed two sweaters, five scarves, and ten pair of gloves. I resisted adding "a partridge in pear tree," but I fear there were many "lords-a-leapin'" among the aristocracy, as they gleefully approved of hanging rebels who had been disloyal to the Crown.

In the years ahead, Fitzgibbon struggled to gain recognition (read: money) for his role in saving the colony of Upper Canada for the British Empire. His requests were ignored. He had won the battles of the rebellion, but lost the fight for a pension.

Meanwhile, the debts of his family increased each year. By 1843, the Bank of Upper Canada threatened court action to force him to repay his outstanding loans. Fortunately, this was never done. Today, the same legal action has been applied to the CEOs of failed American banks. However, Fitzgibbon had title to a piece of land on Queen Street, a short distance to the west of Brock Street (Spadina Avenue). He built a home on this site for his wife, Mary, and their children. The dwelling was only a few minutes' walk from the St. Andrew's Market, close to McDougall's Lane.

Henry Scadding's book, *Toronto of Old*, Toronto, Oxford University Press, 1966, contains a brief description of the house. It reflects Fitzgibbon's financial difficulties.

> A modest dwelling-place of wood—somewhat peculiar in expression; square, and rather tall for its depth; of dingy hue; its roof four-sided; below a number of lean-to's and irregular extensions cluttering round; in front of low shrubbery, a circular drive, and a wide, open-barred gate. This is the home of one who has acquired a distinguished place in our local annals, military and civil.

This sounds like the beginning of Queen Street as a funky, proudly dilapidated streetscape. Had Fitzgibbon been more enterprising, he would have opened a psychedelic coffee shop with a sleazy barroom at the rear and sold "aromatic grass." His financial woes would have been solved.

*

Events in Canadian history continued to roll forward. During the 1850s, Etienne Cartier and John A. Macdonald joined forces to form a coalition government. This was a wise move, as it allowed the future Highway 401 to be named after them—the Macdonald-Cartier Freeway—since renamed the Freedom Highway.

Finally, it was said that Queen Victoria threw a dart at a map of Canada and it pricked a secluded spot on the Ottawa River. Of course this was not true, but it is true that the nation has been tossing darts at Ottawa ever since. Besides, any city that is located in the same province as Toronto is never to be trusted.

We all know what happened during the decade of the 1860s.

A group of men met behind closed doors in Charlottetown, Prince Edward Island, to discuss joining the British American colonies into a political union. They convinced Nova Scotia, New Brunswick, Lower Canada, and Upper Canada to join into a single union.

Because of their skilful negotiations, and because in those days there were no condoms, they all became Fathers ... of Confederation.

Their labours gave birth to a new nation, the Dominion of Canada. The governments of today inherited the methods of the Fathers of Confederation, and developed their skills of secrecy to unfathomable heights. They conceive laws, draft parliamentary bills, and dole out cash in a mysterious manner. They seem to believe that it is better if the people who supply the money do not know how or where it is spent.

As this narrative has inflicted sufficient damage upon the history of Toronto, it is time to bring down the curtain before the censors ban it. We will now seriously examine several of Toronto's historic districts—the "Villages Within."

The Methods Employed in Researching "The Villages Within"

When I was a child in grade four, my teacher inspired in me an interest in history and maps. As a young man, I chose to be an elementary school teacher, then taught secondary school history, and eventually instructed aspiring teachers in curriculum development and methodology in social studies.

When I travelled to Europe in the 1960s, I purchased the tourist guidebooks and read the excellent walking tours that cities offered. When I returned home, I searched for similar resources in Toronto. Alas, I discovered that almost nothing was available. It seemed as if Torontonians believed that their city was not worthy of examination in this manner.

In the late 1960s, I conducted walking tours of the city's historic areas for university students who were taking my course in teacher education. I was amazed by the level of interest. For them, it seemed that history was alive, even when we visited the Necropolis Cemetery, where many of Toronto's important historical personages were buried.

"Digging up history" acquired a new meaning.

When I retired, I was fortunate to relocate to Toronto's downtown area in the one of the oldest districts in the city. The story of Toronto's past surrounded me. It was akin to walking through the pages of a vibrant tale that had not yet been fully written.

This book is a result of the influence of my grade-four teacher, the elementary and high school students who endured my history lessons, and finally, the young student teachers who shared their enthusiasm with me as they accompanied me on walking tours. I am grateful for all of their input.

*

I began by walking the various neighbourhoods that I wished to study, compiling a list of the factories and commercial buildings that interested me. If a house caught my attention, I examined it in detail—dormers, windows, chimneys, and roof, as well as its veranda and the number of storeys. I also recorded the building style, the architectural ornamentation, and the size of the property, including the backyard. In addition, I found it useful to consider the other dwellings and buildings on the street to determine the context of the home.

After a year of on-site exploration, I was ready to commence researching. I journeyed to the City of Toronto Archives and the Toronto Reference Library. I feared that my eyes would suffer from the many hours I spent peering at documents and microfilms. The amount of information available was overwhelming.

In the Toronto Reference Library, I pored over the Toronto directories, which listed the various homeowners, their occupations, family members residing with them, and the year of their construction. When I knew the occupation of a homeowner, the "Names" section of the directories provided the addresses of the various employers. The directories also revealed the changes that occurred over the years to the names of the streets.

The assessment roles in the Toronto Archives revealed the original selling prices of the homes, their assessed value, the size of the building lots, and sometimes the names of the builders.

I employed a similar approach when researching the shops of Queen Street West and the commercial buildings and factories in the Kings West District.

By now, despite the joy of discovery, I was almost ready to crawl into an historic plot within the Necropolis Cemetery and pull the soil over me. However, I recovered after a resurrecting glass of embalming fluid, grenadine, and orange juice, better known as a tequila sunrise.

The interesting part of the project now commenced. For each home I had researched, I combined the data from all sources to create a detailed description of the dwelling. For the factories, I researched the companies and the owners of the businesses. Combining the data, I attempted to reconstruct the lives of the people who either lived in a house or owned a factory or business.

In adopting this speculative approach, I departed from producing an academic study, as much supposition was involved. I felt as though I were a detective investigating cold cases, resurrecting stories from the past.

For example, if a man lived in the Kensington Market area and was employed by a lumber company on Bay Street, it seemed safe to assume that he walked to work. In addition, I was able to determine the possible routes he tread each workday and the sights he passed along the way. The assessed value of his home reflected his position within the company. If the price of his home was high, it was likely that he was in a management or supervisory position, as a labourer would not have been able to purchase and maintain such a costly property. Of course, there was also the possibility that he was living beyond his means, or he had a rich mother-in-law. Thus, this study was not always based on proven facts as I was making educated guesses.

In compiling each profile, I considered the living conditions during the specific decade when the family dwelt in the house—for example, the economic slump during the 1870s. Then I added applicable research gleaned from previous projects, involving the social and political history of the times.

I considered inserting a dictionary of architectural terms but decided to explain the terms to readers as they occurred in the study. A formal bibliography seemed redundant, as the study mainly consisted of archival research, supplemented by my theories and deductions, as opposed to published books. However, when direct quotes were employed, I included the sources.

In some instances, present-day owners of the houses allowed me to view the interior of their homes. I truly appreciated these visits.

I consulted maps in the Goad's Atlases in the Toronto Reference Library to research the public parks, churches, schools, and other public facilities that existed during the years a family lived in a house. For any given decade, these maps also indicated the number of empty building lots on the street, as these were the open areas where the children kicked a ball and played other games. All these observations added to my understanding of what it was like to live within these historic residences and neighbourhoods during the nineteenth century.

It is sincerely hoped that the reader will receive as much enjoyment from the results of my research and deductions as I received from adopting the role of historic detective.

If I have misrepresented any of Toronto's early-day residents, I deeply apologize. My intentions were honourable, as the young romantic interloper said to the virgin maiden.

Chapter Two:

The Historic St. Andrew's Market

This market area is located between Maude and Brant Streets, with Richmond Street West on the north and Adelaide Street on the south.

The West City Market

During the late 1830s, it was becoming obvious that the St. Lawrence Market would be too distant to serve the needs of the residents of Toronto, who were increasingly building homes to the west of Peter Street. As a result, they planned a new market square, the land grant dated May 22, 1837. The northern end of the square was to be 337 feet long, fronting on Richmond Street, and the depth was to be 173 feet. The site consisted of one and three-quarters acres.

On the east, the boundary was Brant Street, with Maud Street on the west, and Adelaide Street on the south. The market was to be named the "West City Market." In 1837, because few residents were dwelling in the area, the creation of the new market square was not a heralded event.

However, the city was continuing to expand westward. Most homes were of wood, but more brick dwellings were being constructed. On Queen Street, to the east of Spadina, rows of two-storey buildings appeared, possessing shops on the street level and residences on the floors above. Along the waterfront were many fine homes. As well, more homes were finally being built in the area surrounding the West City Market Square.

The West City Market Is Renamed St. Andrew's Market

It is not certain when the citizens of York commenced attending the market in the square created in 1837. However, it is likely that sometime during the 1840s, a small seasonal market was held on Saturday mornings, attended mostly by women, as the majority of the men were required to work at their places of daily employment, Saturday being a workday.

Slowly the market grew in size, and in 1850, the city hired the architect Thomas Young to design a frame building to protect shoppers from the weather. Young, born in England in 1805, had previously designed King's College, Toronto, and the wooden building for the St. Patrick's Market on Queen Street.

Maps of the period reveal that the wooden St. Andrew's Market building was constructed in the centre of the market square and contained generous interior space for stalls. A police station and a fire bell were also located within the building. Along the outside walls were produce stands, with canvas awnings sheltering the patrons from the hot summer sun and the rains of spring and autumn, as well as the snows of winter. At the south end of the square, on Adelaide Street, they erected a shelter to protect the horses from the elements. The remainder of the square was green space to accommodate carts, wagons, and the Saturday-morning shoppers. Friends greeted friends, in the background the sound of neighing horses and rumbling wagon wheels.

In 1857, they changed the name of the market to St. Andrew's Market, as the site was in St. Andrew's Ward, Queen Street being the northern boundary line. There were now three markets within the city, the other two being the St. Lawrence (1803) at King and Jarvis Streets and the St. Patrick's Market (1836) on Queen Street, between McCaul and John Streets. The St. Lawrence Market remains popular today, and the St. Patrick's Market still exists on Queen Street West, although the present building dates from the year 1912.

St. Patrick's Market was eventually renamed the Queen Street Market. The small square to the north of the market building retains the former name of St. Patrick's. During warm weather, people sit in this secluded park to drink coffee, chat, or suck on tobacco smoke. Others enjoy a sandwich or slice of pizza. From the square, a little of the Toronto of old remains visible, the houses and laneways clearly portraying the historic lineage of the area.

In 1857, only the St. Lawrence, at King and Jarvis streets, exceeded the importance of the St. Andrew's Market. On a busy Saturday morning, the carriages and horses, as well as the numerous carts of the citizens of Toronto, crowded St. Andrew's Market. It was a gathering place to socialize and chat with friends and neighbours. Housewives purchased vegetables, grains, meat, and fish.

A resident of Toronto wrote, "At Christmas time, the abundance of the market would do credit to any city in the world."

Though this was exaggeration, it expressed the writer's pride as he gazed at the abundance, where many rows of dressed fowl hung from numerous poles suspended above the stalls and shops, whole pigs and sides of beef adding to the display. Counters with an array of beef, pork, and lamb greeted the eyes, alongside baskets of fresh eggs. Bushels of root vegetables were positioned side by side and in some shops were stacked against the rear walls. At Christmas, even the fish stalls managed to display fresh product.

It was an amazing Yuletide scene.

*

During the 1850s, the city continued to push its boundaries westward toward the garrison at Fort York, and the area around the St. Andrew's Market developed rapidly. As a result, a small street was cut through the fields opposite the market, extending eastward from Brant to Spadina, between Richmond and Adelaide Streets. It was surveyed for plot lines to permit homes to be built. This was the creation of Camden Street as we know it today.

The name Camden was derived from Camden Town, a suburb of London, England, formerly named Kentish Town. In 1795, the town had been renamed after Earl Camden, who had died the previous year. He had inherited the manor house at Kentish Town and had been the dominant landowner in the area.

Because many of the immigrants who came to Canada were of British ancestry, place names from the Old Country were frequently transplanted to the young new land. It was in this manner that our illustrious street of Camden was named, after someone who had never accomplished anything of importance or had any claim to fame other than his title. Sounds like a modern Canadian political success story. However, in all honesty, we have likely all heard about a lord or two who accomplished very little, and whose wives were certainly no "ladies."

It is likely that they constructed Camden Street in 1854 or 1855, as the city map of 1853 depicts no such street. The city directory reveals that there were no homes prior to 1855. The earliest house constructed on the street was at 50 Camden. The small home was positioned at the southeast corner of the property where the present-day condominium 50 Camden Street is located. Photographs reveal that the house was a small wooden one-storey home with a gabled roof. Behind it were several outbuildings and a garden of considerable size. By 1866, there were nine houses on the north side of Camden, and ten on the south.

On the southwest corner of Camden and Spadina was Temperance Hall. Today the Fashion Building occupies the site. We can only wonder if the occupants of the offices are aware that they work on a location that once preached the ideals of a non-alcoholic life.

Such a thought is sufficient to drive a person to drink.

The condominium 50 Camden Street, built on land once owned by James Fitzgibbon, hero of the War of 1812.

*

In 1860, the St. Andrew's Market building, located in the centre of the square, was destroyed by fire.

> A few minutes before twelve on the night of December 26, Acting Sergeant Dunlop observed flames bursting through the roof near the centre of the building, and ran to the spot, accompanied by several constables. An attempt was made to get at the fire bell, but the intense

heat rendered this impossible. The attention of the people and the constables was then turned to saving anything they could, and they succeeded in getting out Sergeant Major Cummin's furniture and books and papers belonging to the police station. Meanwhile, the engines arrived, but all their efforts to subdue the flames proved futile and the building was completely destroyed. The building cost five thousand dollars in 1850, and was the property of the corporation. Origin of the fire was not known.

Robertson's *Landmarks of Toronto,*
J. Ross Robertson,
Volume 2,
Mika Publishing, Belleville,
1987 (originally published 1896).

Throughout the 1860s, once more the St. Andrew's Market operated as a seasonal open-air market. In 1873, a handsome grand hall was finally erected. It was an attractive building of white brick, designed in the Renaissance style and appropriately named "St. Andrew's Hall." The former building had been located in the centre of the square, but the new structure was erected at the north end of the property, fronting Richmond Street. A civic ball was held to recognize its opening. Ladies in formal long dresses and elegant gentlemen in frock coats attended. It was a long-remembered gala.

In the modern era, in this area, monkey howls, thumping music, and cries of "ecstasy" from the nightclub crowd are heard on the wee hours of a Sunday morning. Somehow, the sounds are not quite as charming as as those in the days of old.

In the September 15, 1875, edition of the *Irish Canadian*, the following ad appeared:

The Committee on Public Markets will receive offers up to Thursday 16 September, at 12 o'clock noon, for the rental for one year of the shops and stores in the New St. Andrew's Market Building, four [of the shops] fronting on Richmond Street, and one situated in the Arcade. Applicants to consider to tender the business they propose to carry on therein. Also, tenders will be received up to the same date for the fitting up of wrought iron standards for the butchers' stalls in the St. Andrew's Market—James Britton, Canadian Market Committee.

In the 1870s, the new market of St. Andrew's was impressive. According to the Toronto directories, in 1876 it contained thirteen butcher shops. By comparison, the St. Lawrence Market boasted twenty-one butchers, as well as seven fruit/grocer vendors and one "eating house." St Patrick's Market on Queen Street contained only four butchers.

In a decade without refrigeration and fast transportation, imported foods were scarce. With a few exceptions, the ships in the harbour and the railway were the only manner of importing goods, necessitating that foods be dried or preserved. Thus, the city's markets relied on the meat and produce of the farms surrounding the city. Other than dried-salted fish, the only fish available were from the nearby streams and the lakes.

If a person visits the St. Lawrence Market of today and views the area where the butchers' stalls are located, he or she would have an idea of how the St. Andrew's Market appeared in the 1870s. Butchers dominated the scene, and their shops were open every day of the week, except Sunday.

On Saturday mornings, farmers from outside the city brought their produce to the market by horse and wagon and occupied the stalls around the outside of the market building, as well as any available space inside, particularly when the weather was inclement. Their tables and stalls would appear similar to the North Building of today at the St. Lawrence Market, where farmers sell jams, preserves, and breads, as well as their fruits and vegetables. St. Andrew's Market also had a general store, supplying packaged and dry goods. It was a noisy, bustling scene, as merchants called out to attract customers to their shops and stalls.

The 1879 Toronto directories lists the following butchers as occupying stalls or shops within the St. Andrew's Market:

- *East Side of the building:*
- shop #1 E. Brown, #4 Walter Tucker, #6-8 Jno Mallen and Company, #12 William Oxenham.

- *West Side:*
- shop #1 Thomas Murray, #3 Scott and West Butchers, #5 J. G. Marriott, #7 vacant, #11 John Chantler, #13 E. J. Firman.

In 1880, the stalls on the east side of St. Andrew's Market contained five butchers, and there were eight on the west side. None of the stalls was empty. In the Annex, attached to the main building, was Police Station Number Three. The manager of the market was Mr. R. Kennedy. The caretaker of the St. Andrew's Hall was James Hughes, who likely lived on the premises.

A Toronto map of the year 1880 depicts the St. Andrew's Hall and a market building extending to the south of the hall, with stalls for the vendors. It also reveals the overhanging eaves along the outside walls, and beneath these were extra stalls where patrons were protected from the weather. Unfortunately, protection from high prices was not guaranteed.

The History of Toronto and York County, in 1885, lists a few of the vendors who occupied stalls in the St. Andrew's Market.

> J.H.C. Brown, butcher, 2 St. Andrew's Market, does a wholesale and retail business: he buys his stock in the country and does his own killing. He employs four hands, runs two waggons, and deals in all kinds of fresh meat, and also sells hams, tongues, poultry, and vegetables in season. He first established at 336 Queen Street West in 1874, moving to the market in 1876.

> John Chanlter, butcher, first established on Queen Street in 1867, and upon opening of St. Andrew's Market he removed to his present location, 11 St. Andrew's Market. He runs one waggon. He was born in Manchester, England, in 1815, and settled in Toronto in 1866.

> William Oxenham, butcher, 12 St. Andrew's Market, 12 St. Andrew's Market, first established business in St. Patrick's Market in 1855, and in 1861 removed to corner of Chestnut and Queen Street, and in 1876 established himself at the present location. He runs one wagon. He was born in Devonshire, England, and settled in Toronto in 1848.[1]

In 1889, a red-brick annex was built to the west of the St. Andrew's Hall, to house shops and stalls selling vegetables, meat, hay, and feed supplies. This was an attempt to lure farmers away from the St. Lawrence Market. ("Scratch-and-save" cards and "two-for-one" sales had not yet been invented.)

In an open area between the hall and Camden Street was a "weigh house" where vendors could verify the weight of the various products that entered the market. Today, the apartments facing west at 50 Camden overlook the spot.

---

1   *The History of Toronto and York County,* vol. C (Blackett Robinson, 1885), 438.

*

In the 1880s, across from the market, on the north side of Richmond Street (today the site of the condominium 550 Richmond), was the first Salvation Army Barracks (Hall) in Toronto. To the west of this was an empty lot, and on the property to the west of this was a small barn. At the rear of the property was a painter's shop. To the west of this was a wool yard, which extended as far as Portland Street. All these sites are contained within the present-day location of the Cityscape Condominiums, at 500 Richmond Street West.

To the east of McDougall's lane, was a coal shed. The laneway still exists, connecting Queen and Richmond Streets. The colourful graffiti on the walls of the buildings delight some and annoy others who pass through the narrow laneway.

Cityscape Condominium at 500 Richmond Street West.

*

Within the St. Andrew's Hall was a branch of the Toronto Public Library. In the assembly hall on the second floor, political meetings and social functions were held. It was an important building of the community and the social centre of the western part of the city. People gathered to listen to visiting vocal soloists, guest lecturers, and politicians, as well as to attend religious gatherings and hear authors or other persons of interest.

However, during the following two decades, the area surrounding the market changed. By the turn of the twentieth century, the St. Andrew's Market was attracting fewer and fewer customers. Many of the homes on Spadina and Queen were being replaced with shops and stores. Each year, fewer merchants and farmers attended, as customers shopped elsewhere.

By the year 1900, the butchers had all departed from the market. In the main building of the market, only two of the interior spaces were occupied. The York Rangers rented one as a storeroom, and the other the Police Patrol Department leased. The once-busy aisles between the shops were strangely empty.

In the Annex, the decline was also visible, as fewer merchants and more businesspersons rented space.

The following information is from the 1900 Toronto directory:

Space #1, Mary Young, dressmaker, #2 Edward O'Donnell, tea, #3 David E. McArthur, #4 storeroom, #5 William George, # 6, Lois Bush, fruits, #7 John Broughton, #8 Mrs. Mary Murphy, #9 John Price, carriage builder, #10 Stove Polishers' Club, #11-13 vacant, #14 West Office, Board of Works, City Council Labour Bureau.

It is interesting to speculate on the risqué activities that might have occurred at shop #10, the "Stove Polishers' Club." Perhaps it was a front for some dubious goings-on. We can only hope!

In the year 1910, no butchers' shops remained within the hall. The rows of shops were devoid of the displays of meats, as shoppers preferred to patronize stylish stores on nearby city streets. The market contained only Police Station Number Three, six fruit vendors, and the City Weigh Scales. Two of the shops were in use as storerooms. In the Annex, most of the space was employed as storerooms. However, there remained a cabinetmaker, a builder, a carpenter, and the shop of Edward O'Donnell, a "seller of teas." In this year, the population of the city was 424,057, but shoppers preferred to purchase their food supplies beyond the walls of the old market.

On May 23, 1912, a plan was submitted to the City Council to demolish the market and replace it with a water works building. The submission was adopted on September 3, 1912. However, the city did not implement the plan for many years.

In 1931, the city's Water Works Department initiated a detailed report on the St. Andrew's Market. This suggests that they were studying the feasibility of converting the building to provide facilities for the department. Today, the report remains in the Toronto Archives. Although they abandoned the idea of recycling the building, the report provides a few details about the old market. It was constructed of nine-inch bricks and was erected with steel beams. The roof beams were forty-seven feet in length, the roof boarding four feet by four and a half feet, with the planking 1.75 inches thick. The coal room and boiler room were in the basement, and the first floor contained storage space, as well as the management offices. A twelve-foot-wide truck door allowed vehicles to deliver goods to the building. A woodworking shop was on the second floor.

In 1932, the city finally tore down the Annex buildings of the St. Andrew's Market. In the months ahead, the once-admired St. Andrew's Hall was also demolished, brick by brick, and the rubble hauled away in trucks. Their demolition likely provided a make-work project for labourers during one of the harshest years of the Great Depression, when over one third of the work force in Toronto was unemployed.

The market, which had once been the city's second largest, disappeared. The Toronto Water Works built a large building on the site. The area to the south of the Water Works Building, they named the St. Andrew's Playground, the first such designation in the city.

St. Andrew's Hall and Market Buildings, in 1931, the trees of the St. Andrew's playground evident on the far right, and the homes at the corner of Brant and Richmond Streets on the far left.

City of Toronto Archives, Fonds 1244, Item 299

The demolition of the St. Andrew's Hall in January of 1932. View looks west along Richmond Street West. A gasoline pump of that era can be seen on the right.
City of Toronto Archives, Fonds 1231, Item 51

The photograph was created by joining two pictures, both taken on January 5, 1932 when the demolition of the St. Andrew's Hall and Market Building was in progress. The view is from the west, and reveals the two-storey market building that extended from the south side of the hall. It contained the vendors' stalls. On the right-hand side of the photograph are the houses at the corner of Brant and Camden Streets, and the Tower Building on Spadina.

City of Toronto Archives, Series 372, Sub-Series 1, items 1076 and 1077

*

Construction of the Water Maintenance Building in May of 1932. Maud Street is on the left (west) side. There is an excellent view of the buildings on Richmond Street.

City of Toronto Archives, Series 372, Sub-Series 1, Item 1117

Water Maintenance Building on Richmond Street West, at the corner of Brant Street. Photo taken on November 19, 1936.

City of Toronto Archives, Series 372, Sub-Series 1, Item 1412

Doug Taylor

The St. Andrew's Market of Old Returns to the Downtown Scene

In June 2009, on the parking lot on the west side of St. Andrew's Playground, a new St. Andrew's Market commenced, and similar to the days of old, shoppers once more walked to the market square to purchase the produce of the countryside. Unconcerned about parking fees, people lingered to converse with their neighbours as they sipped coffee or hot soup. The revival of the St. Andrew's Market was the result of a group of community residents who volunteered their time to make it a reality.

**A busy Saturday morning in June at the historic
St. Andrew's Market of today, on Adelaide
Street, between Maud and Brant Streets.**

Photo courtesy of Sandy Kemsley

Local restaurants and shops generously provided cooking demonstrations and samples of food. These included Tutti Matti on Adelaide Street West, as well as the Leslieville Cheese Market, Ultra Supper Club, and the Venezuelan restaurant Arepa Cafe, all on Queen Street West. In addition,

George Brown College (Culinary Division) and the Thai Cultural Association contributed. La Merceria, at Adelaide Street West and Maude Street, served delicious hot coffee every Saturday morning.

Rodney's Oyster Market on King Street West generously provided space for the market committee to hold meetings and served pumpkin soup on the Thanksgiving weekend. Apple Self Storage allowed the committee to use one of their lockers to store the table as well as the canopy used by the market volunteer group. The market was a community endeavour, and was once again a focal point in the neighbourhood.

By restoring a tradition of old, a new and vibrant shopping venue was added to the community.

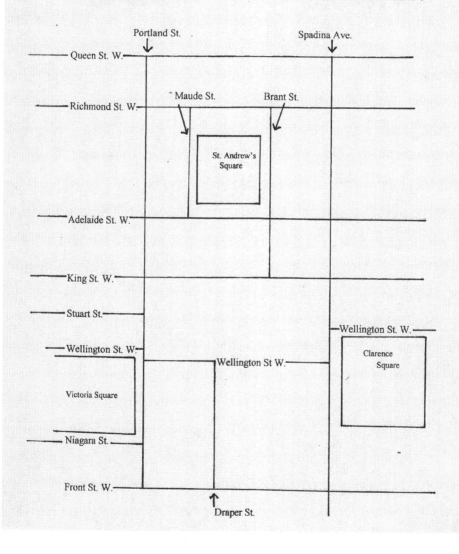

THE SPADINA AND KINGS WEST DISTRICT OF TORONTO

Chapter Three:

The Kings West District

Recent planning documents of the city of Toronto refer to the community that centres on King Street West and Spadina Avenue as the Kings West District. The Kings East District is located around King Street East and Parliament Street.

This study commences at St. Andrew's Playground (refer to map on previous page).

Houses on the corner of Brant and Camden Streets, on December 3, 1937. The homes were demolished in 1940 to create a parking lot. The condominium 50 Camden Street is located on the site today.

City of Toronto Archives, Series 372, Sub-Series 33, Item 263

#43 Brant Street, on the southeast corner of Brant
and Camden Streets, on December 3, 1937.

City of Toronto Archives, Series 372, Sub-Series 33, Item 0264

The intersection of Adelaide Street West and Brant Street,
looking west along Adelaide Street. The schoolyard of Brant
Street Public School, as well as the trees of the St. Andrew's
Playground are evident. Photograph was taken in July of 1958.

City of Toronto Archives, Series 372, Sub-series 100, Item 245

25 Brant Street

Located on the east side of the square is Brant Street, a short distance to the south of Adelaide Street West.

The builders erected this charming warehouse in 1914, for the Canadian Hotpoint Electric Heater Company, whose manager was E. Falcenberg. The west façade is red brick, but the north and south walls are yellow brick. The alternating brick patterns at the corners of the building are referred to as quoins. On the south corner, they are mostly covered over.

The building's simple lines and unadorned façade create a gem of early-twentieth-century industrial architecture. The plain black cornice (trim at the top of the building) contains modillions, which take the shape of over-sized dentils, resembling large teeth.

In the laneway on the north side remains the steel girder that accommodated the pulley that hoisted heavy loads in and out of the factory. With a little imagination, it is possible to envision the horse-drawn carts delivering goods to the loading doors.

In yesteryear, workers chatted amiably as they unloaded supplies that were necessary for the assembly of electric heaters and hoisted the finished products out of the warehouse to awaiting wagons. Most of the deliveries were accomplished by horse-drawn carts, but increasingly trucks, with their square-shaped cabs, were appearing at the factory doors.

The year they built this warehouse, the First World War commenced. News from the trenches of Belgium occupied much of the conversation of the workers. Many of the men had sons or brothers serving in the armed forces. The factory workers who laboured here were to observe many changes in Toronto during the next few years. After the war, life was never again to be the same.

Pause and gaze down the narrow laneway, where the old pulley hangs forlornly, high above the ground. It once looked down upon workers who busily earned a day's wages, while the war reverberated within their thoughts. The echo of the men's voices has long since departed, but the small laneway where they laboured remains, evidence of their passing.

The timeworn phrase "If bricks could talk" is perhaps not a cliché in reference to this venerable old building.

**The factory of the Hotpoint Electric Heater
Company at 25 Brant Street.**

Brant Street School, 20 Brant Street

This well-proportioned rectangular building, constructed in 1926, has a plain façade containing restrained decorative details and stone trim. Brick pilasters (fake columns) adorn the simple façade, beginning at the second floor and extending upward to the third floor. The simple cornice (trim) at the top of the building is copper, which has turned green with age.

Near the top, at both ends of the structure, are designs that resemble warriors' shields, with scrolls on either side, as well as eight round medallions, each with concentric circles. The rear of the building lacks these decorative details.

The spacious rectangular windows permit copious daylight to enter the classrooms, allowing pupils to perform their schoolwork. Though they have modernized the frames of the windows, they have maintained the multi-paned design of yesteryear, and retained the large cement sills.

The heavy, wooden door at the northeast corner appears to be the original. The rods with the hooks that hold the doors open are evident on either side of the doorways. At the corners of the large, arched doorway are quatrefoil designs, found in Gothic windows of the late mediaeval ages. They resemble a four-leaf clover surrounded by a circle. The doorway on the south side of the building is where the pupils would have entered, as it faces the schoolyard.

When this school opened in 1926, it was in the heart of a vibrant residential community. The 1920s was an era when families were larger than today, and the school housed a considerable student body. Compared to the high-tech educational environment of today, teaching was basic, with emphasis on reading, writing, and arithmetic. The teachers maintained strict discipline, and expected the children to conform to the academic standards and strict codes of behaviour. The sturdy, no-nonsense architecture of the building reflected this practical approach to education.

In this decade, students laboured long hours with straight-nib pens to improve their penmanship. If the teachers considered their work exceptional, they might submit it in the contest held each year by the Canadian National Exhibition. The Art and Crafts Building displayed the winners' works at the annual late-summer fair.

When completing penmanship assignments, the only sounds in the classrooms were the scratching of the pen nibs and the ticking of the old clock with Roman numerals, mounted on the rear wall. If an opportunity presented itself, few boys were able to resist the temptation to dip the pigtail of the girl seated in the desk in front of him into the inkwell on his own desk. Only the fear of the teacher's punishment served as a deterrent to his mischievous actions.

In each of the approved readers, inside the front covers was a regal photograph of King George V, with many of the pictures having penciled-in cigars hanging from the mouth of the monarch. A few had added pigtails on the king, with girls' ribbons attached.

Despite the strict discipline of the teachers, disrespect for authority always managed to surface. It was common to find rude poems scribbled on the washroom walls, denigrating the reputation of an unpopular member of staff. These antics are timeless and appear in schools today.

In one cubicle in the washroom, a pupil might have written poetic graffiti that would have shocked Brant Street's prim Miss Dingwall, if she had existed:

Miss Dingbat's full of history,
As full as she can be.
She killed the Roman soldiers,
And now she's killing me.

Gazing inside the classrooms at Brant Street School today, we can view the large classrooms. In the 1920s, these rooms often accommodated thirty-five to forty pupils. The ceilings are high, and old-fashioned lighting fixtures still hang from the ceilings.

The graduates of yesteryear likely insist that they received a better education than "the young people do today." They ignore the exacting demands that the system placed upon them. Many things appear better and gentler in retrospect.

By modern architectural standards, the school may appear as a relic from an old prison movie. However, brick walls do not a prison make. Any building where new ideas are presented and debated is capable of transforming mere mortar and lumber into a learning environment that transcends the most modern computer technology.

Though the echoes of past students no longer haunt the hallways of Brant Street School, it remains lively, as today it houses alternative programs for the Toronto Board of Education, providing interesting and supportive courses for students.

Brant Street School, c.1927. The houses on Brant Street (now demolished), to the south of the school are evident.

City of Toronto Archives, Series 1057, Item 209

To the south of the school is King Street

Every country employs favourite names in its towns and cities to identify its roads and avenues. In Britain, it is unusual to find a hamlet that does not have a High Street. In the United States the names Lafayette, Washington, and Lincoln, or simply Main Street were popular. In Canada during the nineteenth century, among the most common were Victoria, Albert, King, and Queen. Toronto's King Street was named after King George III (1738–1820). Horse-drawn streetcars appeared on the street in 1861, the fare being five cents. The streetcars were electrified in 1892.

On this section of King Street West, the historic factories and warehouses have been restored and are now prestigious offices and retail space.

This section of King Street between Spadina Avenue and Brant Street is reputed to be one of the finest examples of early twentieth-century commercial/industrial architecture in all of North America.

**King Street West on April 13, 1937, looking
west from Spadina Avenue**

**City of Toronto Archives, TTC Fonds, Series 71, Item 4212
Photo Courtesy of the Toronto Transit Commission**

*

511 King Street West, South Side,
Slightly West of Brant Street
The address is visible above the door on the east side.

This Richardsonian Romanesque structure, built in 1893, is a solid, fortress-like building. It was originally the American Watch Case Company, owned by George W. Guinlock. Today, gazing at its impressive façade, it is possible to catch a glimpse of the "ideal" attributes of industrial architecture of the final decades of the nineteenth century and early decades of the twentieth—strength, power, discipline, and respect for the classical traditions.

These sentiments were the hallmark of the British Empire, which was at its height when this building was constructed. Torontonians were fiercely loyal to the sentiments of Empire, and the owners of the American Watch Case Company believed that their premises would inspire customers to patronize their establishment. The building almost screams, "God Save the King, who rules an empire that similar to this building, will never fall."

54

The framework of the building is cast iron, with black cast-iron pilasters (fake columns) on the first level. Large blocks of Credit Valley limestone pilasters anchor either end of the building. The maroon-coloured wooden trim above the first floor has dentils (teeth-like patterns), as well as the Greek egg-and-dart pattern. The windows become progressively smaller with each floor, an attempt to create the appearance of extra height.

The second-floor windows have large blocks of stones inserted above the lintels (top of the windows), similar to some of the windows at Toronto's old city hall.

The architect topped the third-floor windows with Roman arches, whereas the fourth floor windows are smaller and rectangular. Inside the entranceway are marble stairs, and the stairwell has solid mahogany trim.

It is one of the finest examples of commercial Richardsonian Romanesque architecture in the city. Henry Hobson Richardson (1838–1896) studied at Harvard and in Paris. He became fascinated by ancient Roman architecture, with its massive walls, large interior spaces, and graceful rounded arches. His adaptation of this style became known as Richardsonian Romanesque, and he influenced many architects during the years ahead.

The old Toronto city hall, designed by E. J. Lennox, is the city's best example of Richardson's ideas. Another is the Gooderham Building, built between the years 1891–1892, at 49 Wellington Street (Front and Wellington Streets).

The Gurney Stove Foundry, 500–522 King Street, Northeast Corner of King and Brant Streets

The magnificent Victorian buildings, constructed of red and yellow brick, are among the oldest industrial structures in the city. The building on the east (closest to Spadina) is the oldest. With a history that spans almost a century and a half, the E. C. Gurney Company, originated in Hamilton, Ontario. Edward and Charles Gurney manufactured stoves and general castings.

When business expanded, the Gurney brothers opened a retail store in Toronto at 91 Yonge Street. Edward Gurney Junior relocated to Toronto to manage the family business in the provincial capital, purchasing a residence at 209 Jarvis Street for his family.

During the 1870s, much of the land along King Street West was vacant, although it was privately owned. Children in the area ran freely in the fields, kicking a ball and shouting to friends to join in their game. In autumn, the grasshoppers flew in clouds as the children raced along the paths among the fields. In winter, they built snow forts, engaged in snowball fights, and employed creative cursing when they received a direct hit in the face.

However, it was soon to change, as they were to bury the natural playground beneath an enormous industrial complex.

Intending to build a factory in Toronto, in 1872, the Gurney Company bought several of the lots on King, west of Spadina, and erected a four-storey building. Located on the east side of the property, its brick walls were particularly attractive, especially the yellow-brick designs above the windows and the yellow-brick pilasters (fake columns) that rise from the ground level to the top of the building. In 1872, the postal address of the factory was 356 King Street, but today it is 500–510 King Street West. They also constructed more buildings to the north of the King Street structures, but they have not survived into the modern era.

In the year that today's 500-510 King Street opened, a newspaper advertisement stated, "Gurney Stove Foundry, manufacturing agent for the famed Buttan Heater."

The business expanded, and in 1887, they constructed a three-storey building, to the west of the original site. Its address today is 522 King Street. A narrow laneway separated the two structures. During the following years, other buildings appeared to the north of the original two, but these have since been demolished.

The buildings suffered throughout the years ahead, and their attractive façades were covered with a tin siding. In the modern era, when its owners decided to restore the buildings, they removed the tin, revealing the attractive brickwork. It now appears as it did in yesteryear. During the restoration, they replaced the cornices on both structures with metal trim.

In the laneway between the two surviving buildings, they have erected a connecting passageway at the second- and third-floor levels. Thankfully, it matches the two earlier buildings. Today, multiple tenants are located within. With its polished original oak floors and massive wood beams of old-growth Canadian pine, it possesses some of the most handsome nineteenth-century rental spaces in the city.

Viewing these restored buildings today, it is difficult to imagine them being a part of a bustling, sooty, industrial complex, with hundreds of workers labouring in hot, fetid conditions to tend the furnaces, shovelling coal to keep the fires alive. It was an era when workers possessed few rights. Wages were poor and hours were long, usually nine or ten hours a day, six days a week. Lung disease and work-related illnesses were common.

To the modern eye, these factories appear pristine and quaint, their pattered brickwork attractive to behold. The massive pine pillars, visible through the windows of the storefronts, inspire awe. No trees remain in Ontario from which to obtain such magnificent giants ever again.

No trace remains of the hardworking labourers who once inhabited these premises. Evidence of their joys and sorrows has long departed the scene. Only the rattle of the streetcars on the street or the shout of a truck driver remind us of earlier days, when this was a busy industrial complex.

The past has departed forever, but evidence of earlier days remains through the presence of these attractive buildings.

The Gurney Iron Foundry building, at the northwest corner of Brant and King Streets.

485 King Street West, South Side of the Street

This forlorn building has suffered badly during the past few decades. Its empty spaces and altered appearance reveal little of its past, when it contained a vibrant factory employing many workers. The premises have had several different owners throughout its existence.

Until 1889, there was no building on the site. It was an open area, where a wood and coal yard was operated by William Spence. A tall wooden fence separated it from the street, and large lettering on the fence advertised the goods for sale within. As in any era, the fence was a target for local graffiti writers. We can imagine the words, "No matter where you be, let your wind break free," scribbled on the recently whitewashed planks.

As well, it is not difficult to envisage two elderly matrons passing by the fence, the rustle of their long dresses audible in the morning air as they strut imperiously along the wooden sidewalk. One of them notices the offensive words, and her nose flies indignantly in the air. Shocked, she gasps for air, wondering what ever happened to dignity and decorum.

It is fortunate that she never lived to see the words and art forms that now adorn the walls of the Graffiti Alley (McDougall's Lane). She would have required oxygen.

In 1890, Daniel Conboy purchased the land, tore down the ignominious fence, and erected a factory specializing in manufacturing carriage tops. It was a convenient location for Mr. Conboy, as his residence was several doors to the west, at 493 King Street West. In 1913, Thomas M. Brown, who lived at 427 Avenue Road, purchased the building. His company was the Independent Cigar Company. The structure possessed large windows, which provided excellent lighting for the workers. Today, most of the windows on the west side have been filled in with concrete blocks. The red bricks have been painted grey, and the storefront on the first floor has been severely altered. A five-foot parapet (a wall at the top of a building with nothing behind it) increases the height of the façade. It is readily evident if a person views the building from the east side. It is necessary to stand back a short distance to see the parapet.

Today, the building remains unoccupied. It is hoped that in the future it will be restored, and once again house a successful enterprise.

469 King Street West, South Side of King Street

The ornate Classic Revival-style factory that stands before you was built in 1903, and was the Dominion Paper Box Company. In 1907, they added an addition at the rear to create extra space for the factory. The four-storey structure is constructed of red brick, the basement partially below ground. Again, they intended the solid-looking building to signify that the company was a well-established, trustworthy business firm.

Despite the impressions created so far in this study, there were indeed disreputable business establishments in this decade. Every era possesses merchants who prize profit above honesty.

Dare I mention the elderly matron who purchased a highly priced corset from a trusted merchant? It was guaranteed to be reliable under the most trying of circumstances. It burst during an exhilarating romantic encounter, the straps strangling her lover and the buttons from the corset shooting the eyes out of her dog. Some said that the dog's fate was a blessing, as it would never again have to endure such a horrific sight.

However, the Dominion Paper Box Company never suffered from the slings and arrows inflicted by such stories. Its noble façade displays much ornamentation, especially the impressive doorway, known as a "Gibbs Surround," named after James Gibb (1672–1754). It consists of large blocks of stone, interrupted by a rounded pilaster (column). A classical egg-and-dart design is under the overhang above the doorway. On either side, small winged cherubs peer out from a spot near the top of the columns. The magnificent doorway dominates the street.

The first-floor level is the most detailed, with three rows of dentils in the trim above it. The floors above are less ornamented. It is one of the finest examples of early twentieth-century buildings in the entire city.

The "Gibbs Surround" that frames the doorway of 469 King Street West.

461 King Street, South Side of King

This factory, with its ornate façade built in 1901, was the premises of the Toronto Lithography Company. At one time, the Salada Tea Company occupied it. Though sometimes criticized for the exuberance of its classical designs, today it provides a pleasant contrast to the sparseness found in the modern architecture that has become prevalent throughout the city.

This factory aptly demonstrates the pride that early nineteenth-century businessmen felt about their businesses, as expressed through architecture. At the top of this red-brick building, under the cornice (moulding at top of building), is a row of dentils, as well as another of the classical Greek egg-and-dart pattern. The modillions (brackets) under the eaves support the cornice. There are simplified Greek Ionic pilasters on either side of the entranceway, with small winged cherubs perched on the top of them. The harsh Canadian winters have eroded some of the details on the cherubs, partially obscuring them. Despite this defect, I do not believe it is proper to refer to them as "fallen angels."

The doors house frosted glass with intricate designs. Inside on the first floor is a small foyer decorated with marble, and the stairs are of the same material. The lobby is spacious, with dark oak panelling. To the right of the lobby is the reception area, which they have carefully maintained throughout the years.

At the beginning of the twentieth century, the company employed it as a grand room to greet clients. It is not difficult to imagine the sense of awe that perspective clients felt when ushered into this spacious room and confronted by the luxurious decor. The plaster ceiling of the room has classical Greek designs and they have adorned the walls with impressive oak wainscoting

A fireplace dominates the south side of the room, creating a welcoming atmosphere, so comforting on gloomy days during a Toronto winter. Many lucrative transactions were completed as they huddled beside its warmth.

459 and 457 King Street West, South Side of King
The entire building was originally numbered 455, but it has been split into two separate addresses.

During the nineteenth century, the Toronto Pharmacal Company operated from a small building on this site. The property was owned by Henry

Sherris, president of the Pharmacal Company, who was also president of the SDS Realty Company. By 1909, he required larger business premises and built the present structure.

The red-brick building has three floors and a basement that is partially above ground. A wide staircase ascends steeply from the first to the top level. On the façade, rounded Roman arches appear above the windows on the third floor, and the second- and third-floor windows have limestone lintels (top of windows). Cement scrolls decorate either side of the doorway. In 1914, it was occupied by the Brangs and Heinrick Paper Company. Its interior spaces, with their exposed brick and enormous pine beams, are much sought-after premises for trendy businesses who wish to attract hip clientele.

The Krangle Building, 445–447 King Street West, South Side, West of Spadina

Despite the name "Krangle" being visible above the doorway, repeated attempts have uncovered no explanation for its origin. It's always interesting to explore a building with a mystery, akin to meeting a lady with a hidden past.

The site was originally a coal and wood yard, but the land was purchased in 1908 by James Brown, who erected the present structure in 1909. He appropriately named it the Brown Building. He operated a small printing business and rented space to other tenants, among them the William Rogers Silverware Company. In 1950, it was bought by the Regent Electric Supply Company and became known as the Regent Building.

The ornate design surrounding the doorway is a "bay leaf garland," with small dentils above the doorway and a row of larger dentils further up. In the black trim above the first floor are more dentils. The original cornice at the top has been replaced with metal trim.

It remains a handsome structure, this mysterious "lady of King Street," retaining her sedate presence on the avenue, easy to gaze upon but difficult to engage in intimacy.

The 1903 Krangle Building at 445–447 King Street West

468 King Street West, North Side of the Street

In 1880, this was the site of the Ontario Cabinet Works, one of Toronto's earliest factories. In 1905, Sigmund Samuel and Frank Benjamin bought the property and constructed a six-storey yellow-brick building with a plain façade, detailed with small blocks of stone and cement.

The first floor has a stone façade. The cornice (at the top) is attractive, with simple designs and shields surrounded by scrolls. The doorway is a Roman arch. A narrow covered carriageway on the east side of the building allowed wagons and trucks from King Street to access the three loading doors at the rear of the building. Though silent today, in the past these doors were constantly thrust open, even on cold winter mornings, to receive goods and ship-out finished products.

It was named the Samuel and Benjamin Building. Inside the small lobby one can see the grand open staircase, a remainder of the days prior to elevators. It commences at the first floor and soars to the sixth. Painted in contrasting colours of white and cobalt blue, it is the most impressive stairwell in the district. If the building is open, it is worthwhile to step inside to view the great staircase and gaze upward at its impressive design.

439, 435, 433, 431, and 425 King Street West, the Samuel Building, Southeast Corner of Spadina and King Street
The building has five doorways on King Street, each with its own address.

This corner property was originally owned by Samuel Richardson, owner of the property on the opposite corner on King Street. He sold the empty field to F. W. Thompson as a site for a coal and wood yard. During this decade, those who passed on the street glimpsed stacks of coal and piles of lumber. It was an era when the homes of Toronto were heated mainly by coal fireplaces or stoves. In winter, a haze of smoke hovered above the city, a dirty blanket of soot particles.

In 1908, brothers Jacob and Sigmund Samuel, along with another investor named Frank D. Benjamin, vice-president of the M. and L. Benjamin and Company, bought the property. They formed a partnership and the new company was named Samuel and M. and L. Benjamin Company, Metals. As they wished to build on the site, they eagerly sought financing. In 1911, they were successful and constructed the six-storey Samuel Building of red brick, which is the structure that you see before you today. It was among the first factory-warehouses built in the city to accommodate multiple tenants, necessitating three separate doorways on King Street. When renovated in the late twentieth century, two more doors were added. The demands of the modern era often force alterations on these proud old buildings. However, it is important that they maintain them despite these changes.

The Samuel Building was constructed prior to the days when elevators were common. The open staircase, which extends from the ground to the top floor, was clearly an attempt to impress visitors. This was especially true if a person stood at the bottom and gazed upward at the marble steps and luxurious wainscoting. On the façade, although there are brick pilasters between the windows, topped at the fifth floor with stone, the north-facing (King Street) side of the building is unadorned, with very few decorative details. Large stone Roman arches sit above the three original doorways.

Today, the building dominates the corner of Spadina and King. It is an architectural gem that remains polished despite the passing years.

It is particularly impressive after the sun sets, as the soft beams of light illuminate the brickwork that was fired in the kilns of the past.

460 King Street West, Northwest Corner of King and Spadina

In 1873, Samuel Richardson erected a two-storey frame home on this corner. It survives today and, though much altered, remains as the heart of the complex. He added a third floor in 1875, built in the Second Empire style of architecture, with a mansard roof and ornate gables. When completed, the premises opened as the Richardson House, a hotel and tavern serving the businessmen of the western part of the city. As Richardson had served for eleven years in foreign lands with the troops of the Thirteenth Hussars, he rarely failed to promote this fact when advertising his establishment.

In 1885, a four-storey brick addition was added to the north side of the hotel, on Spadina Avenue, and two years later another extension was added, doubling the number of rooms. The hotel advertised hot water heating in every room, for the low rate of $2.00 per day. Weekly boarders received a special rate of $1.50.

Samuel Richardson died in 1904, and in 1906 the premises were renamed the Hotel Falconer. Its name was changed again in 1914, when it became Zeigler's Hotel, and in 1916, it was the Spadina Hotel. In the 1950s, the large room on the second floor, on the north side of the hotel, was redecorated and named the Cabana Room. It became a centre for the avant-garde creative community of the city.

Established artists and students from the Ontario College of Art (today the Ontario College of Art and Design) congregated in the Cabana room to raise a glass to toast their accomplishments or to drown the disappointment of their failures. These students vilified, praised, defended, and ignored the latest trends in art. Throughout the decades ahead, many of the young artists established themselves in promising careers in galleries, graphic design firms, and commercial art establishments. Others, just like the old hotel, fell into obscurity. Such is the way of life in the creative community. Today, the owners have employed the second-floor Cabana Room for other purposes.

During the 1950s, they restored the first-floor dining room to its 1883 splendour, with Canadian walnut and chestnut panelling. If a person enters the hotel today and walks to the far end of the lobby, there is a narrow set of stairs with five steps, which leads to what was once the dining room. The old doors and the wood panelling remain, but the space is now a billiard and games room, much removed from its elegant past. Today, the glorious old hotel is a hostel for student backpackers, with 185 beds available and four occupants per room. Because of the building's brightly coloured walls, ornate gables, and garish trim, it is a landmark in the Spadina district.

One hopes that its uniquely saucy architecture never disappears from the downtown urban scene.

The Samuel Richardson house, now a part of a small hotel complex, on the southwest of King Street West and Spadina Avenue.

**The corner of King Street and Spadina Avenue
c. 1900, looking west along King Street.**

City of Toronto Archives, Fonds 1568, Item 282

Clarence Square, South of King Street, on the East Side of Spanida Avenue

The open green space, named Clarence Square, on the east side of Spadina Avenue, opposite Wellington Street West, was at one time a part of the military reserve attached to Fort York.

In the 1830s, British engineers created it to form an important part of a lakeside promenade. During those years, the shoreline of Lake Ontario was on the south side of Front Street, but in the years ahead landfill pushed the lake farther south. Today, Clarence Square is isolated from the water, but it remains a small charming park, its giant trees providing a quiet retreat in the heart of the city, secluded from the heat of the summer sun.

It is reminiscent of squares created in London, England, during the 1820s. The wide avenues, with vistas terminating in large public open spaces, were known as the Regency style. Regent Street in central London is perhaps the best-known example. The design was later promoted in Canada by amateur architects such as William Warren Baldwin.

Several sources consulted for this study stated that the square was named after Albert Victor, Duke of Clarence (1864–1892), eldest son of Edward VII. However, the name Clarence Square appears on the city maps of the 1850s, before Albert Victor was born. It is more likely that the square received its name from the third son of King George III, Prince William Henry, born in 1765. In 1789, the king granted him the title Duke of Clarence and St. Andrew's. The duke served in the Royal Navy and became admiral of the fleet in 1811. He ascended the throne as King William IV, and died on June 20, 1837. This was the decade when Clarence Square was created by the British troops from Fort York, and it was likely named in his honour. William IV was succeeded on the throne by his niece, Elizabeth Victoria, and the Victorian era was born.

Most sources that record the history of Clarence Square and Wellington Place (now Wellington Street West) offer the opinion that they fell short of their potential and never developed as they were envisioned. However, if we examine old maps of the city, it seems that this is not truly accurate. Mansions and estates did indeed appear on Wellington Place, and lined both sides of the avenue. Spacious grounds and ornate gardens surrounded them. Unfortunately, they were destroyed in the twentieth century during the street's transition from residential to industrial/commercial.

The same is true for Clarence Square. Two of the grandest houses ever constructed in Toronto were situated on the square. On the north side at number 304 was the home of Hugh John Macdonald, son of Sir John A. Macdonald, the nation's first prime minister. On the south side of the square at number 303 was the residence of John Gordon, a magnificent mansion in the detailed Italianate style. Gordon was a very wealthy man who had acquired a fortune importing dry goods. He became the president of the Toronto Grey and Bruce Railway. These two houses had sufficient space surrounding them that it was not possible to build more houses on the square. In the centre of the square was an ornate fountain. It was truly a prestigious area during those years.

To the south of his residence, John Gordon owned a tract of land, which he sold it to the railway to allow the company to build train tracks on the south side of Front Street. Within a year or two, because of the noise and soot of the steam engines, Clarence Square was no longer viewed as desirable, so the house was sold and eventually demolished. Macdonald's home, on the north side of the square, disappeared in the late 1870s, and in its place a row of houses was built in the Second Empire style. The bricks of these historic residences are today hidden beneath grey stucco. Most of them are now offices.

It is a pity that there is no historic plaque to commemorate the history of the square. The plaque that exists in the northwest corner honours Alexander Dunn, who in 1854 was the first Canadian recipient of the Victoria Cross. There is a plan to redevelop this old square, and perhaps they will correct this deficiency.

Clarence Square, looking east from Spadina
Avenue, October 19, 1913.

City of Toronto Archives, Series 372, Sub-series 52, Item 198

Wellington Street West, West Side of Spadina Avenue

As one looks westward from Spadina to Portland, it requires a great leap of imagination to visualize Wellington Street as it appeared in yesteryear. When they originally surveyed the land, they created large building lots, with thirteen on the north side of the street and seventeen on the south.

The avenue was one hundred feet wide, with rows of ornamental trees on either side, creating a grand pedestrian promenade. It was a favourite avenue for citizens to stroll along, meet friends, and greet neighbours. Each year this began in earnest on the first sun-filled days of early spring, and lasted until the chill of late autumn forced residents to seek comfort beside their fireplaces. The majestic trees flanking the roadway provided cool shade for the pedestrians and carriages that frequented the area. The two public squares anchoring either end of the street added to the avenue's appeal. It was a prestigious location, a worthy site for those wealthy enough to live there. A few citizens purchased multiple lots to allow sufficient space for larger dwellings.

The following information is from the Toronto Assessment Rolls of 1892. It lists the occupations of the residents of Wellington Street, then known as Wellington Place. It is evident that they possessed considerable financial means and were prominent members of the community.

The occupations of the inhabitants are listed as follows: gentleman, bank executive, barrister, merchant, architect, sheriff of York County, insurance executive, boiler and engine manufacturer, surgical instrument manufacturer, and accountant.

There were three estates on this section of Wellington Street. J. Dent's property was surrounded by a red-brick wall, six feet high on the front and sides of the property and ten feet at the rear. Another of the mansions was owned by Charles Mitchie, who earned his living selling wholesale groceries and imported wines. His company was located at 7 King Street West. On the third estate lived H. L. Hime. He was listed on the assessment rolls as a "gentleman," meaning that he likely had inherited his wealth or retired following a successful business career. These men attempted to emulate the style of living of the great homes in the English countryside. They constructed out-buildings on their estates, which sometimes included greenhouses, stables, carriage houses, smoke sheds, and sometimes cottages for the servants.

Unfortunately, these estates have all disappeared, because as the century progressed land values steadily increased and the large properties became very expensive to maintain. In the mid-nineteenth century, the railway arrived in Toronto, constructed on land to the south of Front Street, only slightly more than a block away from Wellington Street. Similar to Clarence Square, families with wealth no longer considered the area desirable.

Eventually, developers purchased the large estates. When the families sold their properties, they relocated further from the downtown core, to the Annex or Rosedale. The Wellington Street homes were demolished and industrial buildings replaced them, taking advantage of the close proximity of the rail lines. None of the estates survived. Although a few of the lesser homes of yesteryear remain, they have been greatly altered.

The Conversion of Wellington Street West from Residential to Commercial

During the early decades of the nineteenth century, merchants required funding to expand their enterprises, so they established banks. With better financing available, they were more successful, and soon outgrew the cramped space within their shops. Larger premises were required to store the increased supply of goods that arrived by ship, and this intensified with the arrival of the railway.

Land near the harbour became ideal for these purposes. In the 1870s, they constructed warehouses along Front Street, on the east side of Yonge Street. Many of these still exist today. During the early years of the twentieth century, the possibilities of the properties along Wellington Street West became evident. As mentioned, when residential owners sold their dwellings, business enterprises purchased the properties, demolished the houses, and built factories and warehouses.

The new warehouses along Wellington Street West were constructed differently from earlier types. They were much larger, and the floors possessed open space that they could alter easily as requirements changed. The high ceilings provided room to stack goods. The concept of warehouse lofts was born. More than one tenant often shared the premises to maximize the use of space and reduce costs.

Before elevators came into use, the most that people were expected to walk up was four floors. However, loft warehouses pushed the limit to five floors. Those built with elevators went a few floors higher. Windows were multitudinous and large. The brick façades were simple in design, containing only a few classical adornments. Pillars were simulated by arranging the bricks in a raised pattern and topping them with cement or stone. Cornice trim on the top was kept to a minimum. Limestone was sometimes employed to enhance the appearance of the ground floors.

These loft warehouses and factories will now be examined, along with the few remaining homes.

376–374 Wellington Street West
Houses beside the service station on the northwest corner of Spadina Avenue and Wellington Street West

Construction of these dwellings commenced in 1888 and completed the following year. They are semi-detached three-storey homes of the bay-and-gable design. In the pediment (peak), there are simple designs cut from wood with a scroll saw. There are large keystones above the windows and heavy stones beneath. Their addresses in that decade were numbers 2 and 4 Wellington Place. These numbers changed when they incorporated Wellington Place into Wellington Street West. The yellow-brick houses originally sold for $3395, located on 19-by-112-foot lots.

Number 376 was first occupied by Mrs. Thomas T. Coyne, a solicitor. Number 374 was purchased by Mrs. E. H. Bethune, the widow of E. H. Bethune Q.C., also a lawyer.

When these prominent families occupied the homes, Spadina Avenue was a relatively quiet thoroughfare. The park (Clarence Square) located on the east side of the avenue was a tranquil, secluded green space where the local children played games and in winter built snowmen. In summer, they slurped a cool drink from the fountain in the centre of the grassy square. Their parents, or an elderly guardian, observed them from the benches located under the shade of the mature trees at the edge of the park. The area was mainly residential in the 1880s, and thus most families living within walking distance frequented the park.

On a quiet summer morning, the heavy clip-clop of a horse pulling a lumbering wagon northward from Front Street drew curious glances. The children wondered what interesting cargo it was transporting from the belly of a sailing vessel moored to the wharf extending into the lake. They usually ignored a southbound wagon, as it invariably contained no goods.

The families who resided at 374 and 376 Wellington Street never dreamt of the momentous changes that the decades ahead would inflict upon their tranquil world.

71

**Two houses at 424 Wellington Street West,
which were constructed in 1889.**

424 and 422 Wellington Street West
(houses with the stone lions)
Both these buildings are today numbered 424.

Today, the office workers, condominium owners, and patrons of the restaurants and clubs mostly ignore these magnificent houses as they pass by on the sidewalks of Wellington Street West. However, in their day, they were two of the finest homes in Toronto.

Constructed of red brick in 1889, these three-storey attached houses possess neo-Tudor wood designs on the bargeboards in the pediments, as well as in the cornice trim along the edge of the roof. They are of heavy black wood, resembling the timbers found in a great hall in an English Tudor palace or mansion. The original slate rock roofs have survived and remain in good condition, but the front doors have been replaced. The porches also have not survived. Majestic lions repose on either side of the stairs, and there is a lion's head in a central position of the façade. Lions' heads also appear in the brickwork above the windows on the first floor. Large brackets support the cornices.

The builder of these houses was James Hewett. In 1889 the selling price was $7600. During this same period, the row houses facing Denison Square were selling for anywhere between $1800 and $2500. Thus, the houses on Wellington Street West were not within the means of the average wage earner. Today, it is difficult to imagine how attractive these dwellings would have appeared when their surroundings were landscaped and the street was a grand tree-lined avenue.

The first resident of number 422 was John C. Smith, the proprietor of Cooper and Smith, Boots and Shoes. Charles Powell was the first occupant of #424. Previously residing in Hamilton, Ontario, he bought the house when he relocated to Toronto. He was the manager of the Temperance Colonization Limited at 124 King Street West. Records do not provide any details of this business, so we are left to speculate as to its purpose. In 1892, Mr. Powell retired from the company, and the city directories simply list his status as being a "gentleman."

On the evenings when these families entertained, the gaslights were visible from the street, filtering softly through the darkness. On these occasions, men and women in formal attire alighted from their horse-drawn carriages, their laughter and animated conversations betraying their excitement at being entertained in such regal surroundings.

Today, the homes appear rather empty and forlorn. The spacious front lawns have been paved over to provide parking spaces. Though not evident from the street, the houses have been combined and are employed as banquet rooms for receptions and weddings. The original marble fireplaces and the staircases with their hand-carved banisters survive, as well as the gas fixtures, although the latter are no longer in use.

The glory days of these homes have long since been spent, but anyone with an imaginative eye can still experience their past importance in the Toronto scene.

436 Wellington Street West, North Side

The six-storey Monarch Building, built in 1914, was originally the Croft Building, factory of William Croft and his son, manufacturers of small wares. Though it has an unadorned façade, similar to other structures on the street, it possesses pilasters, in this instance capped with limestone.

There is also limestone on the first-floor level. On the east side of the building, all the windows except one have been bricked over.

Today, the Monarch Building has been converted into spectacular open-planned condominiums that have penthouse apartments with garden terraces. The lobby retains the original marble, as well as the pine beams and wood ceiling. A handicap elevator has been installed, and on the west side, the loading door has been altered to create a second entranceway for the residents.

The present-day owners are fortunate to live in a landmark building that retains its rich historic past.

439 Wellington Street West, South Side

In 1915, the Victoria Paper and Twine Company, a textile manufacturer, built this three-storey yellow-brick building. It shared the premises with R. G. Long and Company, a manufacturer of gloves.

This structure, one of the most interesting on the street, has generous wood trim on the façade, which today, they have painted a dark red. The second- and third-floor levels have columns consisting of alternating layers of brick and stone. The loading doors remain visible at the front of the building, on the right-hand (west) side. Large windows allow the interior to be brightly lit with natural light. The name of the original owner is carved in the stone above the impressive doorway, which has old oak doors, with transom and large side-light windows. At the top of the building, the cornice has been removed and replaced with grey metal.

It is not known why the initials HSH were carved in the stone on the left side of the doorway. The building is another architectural lady with a hidden past.

The Victoria Building, 439 Wellington Street West.

462 Wellington Street West, North Side

Built in 1916, this building housed the Houlding Knitwear Company. In its day, the public considered the structure's design a "modern" classic, with its simple façade and smooth limestone base. When it opened its doors in 1916, the employees who entered its precincts were proud to work in one of the architectural marvels of the era, similar to those in the modern era who first passed through the doors of the Toronto-Dominion Bank Centre on King Street. Though such buildings change through the years, the "pride of presence" often remains.

The Houlding Knitwear building has slender brick pilasters that ascend to the fifth floor. The design of the entrance is plain, with inset oak doors, while the windows on the second floor have detailed stone adornments under the sills. The loading door, which was on the east side of the building, they have bricked over.

Two buildings at 488 Wellington Street West.

488 Wellington Street West, North Side, Opposite Draper Street

At this site are two five-storey, open-spaced, red-brick buildings joined to create a single complex. The bricks on the eastern building are a brighter colour of red than is its mate. The latter was built in 1908 by Mendel Granatstein, who, with his sons, operated a salvage and waste management company. Their business was very successful, and ten years later more space was required.

In 1918, a new building was constructed on the west side of the original. It contains simple brick patterns on the façade and pilasters topped with small domes. In the decade when it was built, the design was greatly admired due to its simplicity. The doorway is impressive, and the first floor has a white limestone cladding. The metal window sashes were among the first installed in Toronto. In the eastern building, there are four brick pilasters on the façade. Two of these are narrow, and two are wider.

Limestone is employed in the sills under the windows, from the second to the fifth floor. The cornice contains the classical Greek egg-and-dart pattern.

Today the buildings are condominiums, with terrace gardens on the apartments' roof. They are excellent examples of refitting early-day buildings to accommodate the needs of the modern era. In so doing, the developer has preserved an architectural gem.

479 Wellington Street West.

479 Wellington Street West
On the south side, northeast corner of Wellington and Draper Street.

When I began the research for this study, I found the origins of this nineteenth-century yellow-brick commercial building, at the southeast corner of Wellington and Draper, a mystery. After several visits to examine it, I found nothing conclusive to reveal its origins. The large porch entranceway facing west on Draper Street, the Gothic windows on the second floor above it, and the Gothic windows on the north façade suggested that at one time it might have been a church. When examining the brickwork of the porch, it was evident that over the years several changes had been made to the structure. The architecture was not typical of Victorian-era houses. It required much research in the archives before its story was revealed.

Finally, I discovered that the structure was built in 1877 as a residence, and at one time was one of the grandest on the avenue. Its dimensions were 88 by 140, and the assessed value of the land and house the year it was constructed was $10,344. It was purchased by William Colwell, a Toronto alderman and wealthy businessman, who earned his living selling lumber. His company was W. W. Colwell and Brother, and the firm sold wood shingles, cedar posts, and lathe work—both retail and wholesale. The yard and offices were located south of the house on Front Street. Coleman's brother Henry also lived on Wellington Street West, next door to his brother and business partner.

In 1883, the house was sold to Francis E. Macdonald, a competitor who was also in the lumber trade. He remained in the residence until 1892, when he rented the premises to Joseph P. Widdifield, the Sheriff of York.

Finally, in 1906 the house at 479 Wellington Street West was sold by Macdonald to George B. Meadows. However, Mr. Meadow's residence was at 6 Sussex Street. He had purchased the dwelling to convert it into a factory for his Toronto Iron and Brass Works Company. To accomplish the adaptation, the original structure was altered, and a red-brick extension was added to the south of it. As well, two structures were added on the east side, on Wellington, to increase the space required for the factory. The peaked roof of the house was removed and replaced with one that was flat, its height level with the new sections.

Today, the quoins (decorative brick patterns at the corners of a building) on the original yellow-brick section reveal the alterations. On this house, red bricks were employed, and in summer, they are visible only on the northwest corner, as they are obscured elsewhere by vines of ivy. The quoins do not ascend fully to the roof line, revealing the bricks that were added when the peaked roof was removed.

Despite the severe changes to the original house, the building that remains on the property is an attractive commercial complex. The exterior of the old house has mostly survived. Facing Wellington Street, the main entrance to the building has an impressive set of blue-grey doors with sidelight and transom windows. The origin of these old doors is unknown.

Draper Street

On Wellington Street West, halfway between Portland Avenue and Spadina Avenue, is Draper Street. It was named after William Henry Draper (1801–1877), a jurist and politician, as well as the chief justice of Upper Canada from 1863 to 1869. His portrait in oils hangs in the library of Osgoode Hall.

The land occupied by Draper Street, once a part of the military reserve attached to Fort York, the city annexed in the 1830s. It appears on the city's maps in the year 1857, although the exact year they cut it through the woods is unknown. In the 1880s, when houses were constructed, it became a working man's community, unlike Wellington Place at its north end.

The following is a list of the occupations of the residents of the street in 1892: telegraph operator, policeman, plumber, bookkeeper, labourer, machinist, insurance agent, jeweller, passenger agent, traveller, painter, printer, fireman, employee of Toronto Water Works, stonemason, clerk, engine driver, tax collector, conductor, and Grand Trunk Railway employee.

With few exceptions, Draper Street retains its nineteenth-century streetscape. In 1984, in celebration of the city's 150th anniversary, the city designated all of the houses as "Heritage Properties." In 1999, the residents applied for "historic designation" and now the façades of the houses cannot be altered without permission. The short street is certainly worthwhile visiting, as it is akin to entering a time tunnel into Toronto's past.

The first houses appeared on the east side of the street in 1881 (numbers 11–29), and on the same side (numbers 3–9) in 1884. In 1886, houses were built on the west side (numbers 4–18). The four southern lots closest to Front Street, two on either side, did not have dwellings until 1887. The two on the west side have since been demolished and replaced by a commercial building of cement blocks. House numbers 19 and 21 were knocked down in the 1930s, as they were in a very poor state of repair. The site where they were located is today a small park. It is used for Draper Street's annual street party. On the west side, at the north end of Draper, there are seven three-storey bay-and-gable homes. They were built in 1890 on the site of Benton's Lumber Yard.

Because most of the houses are either small, two-storey workmen's houses with mansard roofs, or tall, three-storey Victorian dwellings similar to row houses, only a few of the residences will be examined in detail.

29 Draper Street

This Second Empire house was built in 1881 by Richard Humphries. It has a mansard roof, but the large bay window on the first floor has been replaced by a brick extension to the living room. Its first resident was Charles Cluthe, a machinist by trade.

The Honourable Lincoln Alexander was born in this house in 1922. He became the first black Member of Parliament in Ottawa, as well as the first black lieutenant governor of Ontario.

22 Draper Street, West Side

This is one of the seven dwellings constructed in 1890 on the site of Benton's Lumber Yard and is an excellent example of Toronto's unique bay-and-gable houses. Number 22 Draper Street was the home and workplace of Miss Annie Riorden, a dressmaker. In this decade, the selection of ready-made dresses available at the dry goods stores was quite limited. Most women purchased material from a bolt of cloth and made their own dresses, as well as those for other members of their families. Ladies who could afford the price employed dressmakers. They chose the material and style, had a fitting, and then had the cutting and sewing done by the dressmaker. Miss Riorden chose an excellent location for her business. The matrons of the mansions on Wellington Place were frequent customers, and the proximity of her home to these residences was a great advantage.

This three-storey narrow house has large bay windows on the first floor that continue to the second-floor level. High in the pediment, the wood trim has simple designs. The original porch-supports remain today, and at the top contain sunburst patterns in the corners, with a row of spindle ornaments produced on a lathe in a lumberyard. The slate roof has not survived.

There is a transom window above the door, as well as a large window in the door itself, allowing copious daylight to enter the hallway within. It was an era before electricity, and without such designs the interior of the house would be very dim, especially during the winter months.

The tall windows were an asset for Miss Riorden as she performed the detailed tasks required to complete the cutting and sewing of a dress. With a little imagination, we can picture her seated beside a large bay window on the second floor, sewing in the morning light. On winter days, perhaps she also had a small work area at the rear of the home to take advantage of the afternoon sun.

18 Draper Street, West Side

This house was built in 1882 by Richard Humphrey, whose construction offices were at 424 Front Street West. Its first resident was John B. Hayes. It changed owners several times, and in 1888, it was purchased by Lucius C. Benton, the owner of the lumberyard who occupied the land to the north between the house and Wellington Street West. In her book *Toronto Architecture*, Patricia McHugh (McClelland and Stewart, Toronto, 1985) described 18 Draper as a "Second Empire cottage, one-and-a-half-storeys high, and sweetly detailed with a bay window and panelled brick."

It is an excellent example of a workingman's home in the Second Empire style, which was very fashionable in France during the reign of Napoleon III (1852–1870). The design came to Canada via the United States. It included mansard roofs in which ornate gables were inserted. In Toronto, during the 1870s, it was popular for public buildings, and in the 1880s, for domestic architecture. In Toronto, many Second Empire houses remain today, scattered throughout the downtown area, including some impressive three-storey dwellings. The George Brown House on Beverley Street and the Beardmore home at the corner of Dundas and Beverley Streets are excellent examples.

Mansard roofs were practical as they provided more space for bedrooms or storage. It was an era when families had many children. In some of the small houses in Toronto, no larger than the homes on Draper Street, there were sometimes as many as twelve children.

Number 18 Draper Street is a cottage-size dwelling. The façade of the second floor retains the original slate tiles. The house was constructed of red bricks and employed yellow bricks for decoration above the door and windows. Similar to its neighbours, there is a transom window above the door. The large bay window on the first level adds to the attractiveness of the home.

17 Draper Street

In 1881, this house was purchased from the builder by J. J. Dyas, an advertising agent, who in that year was twenty-three years old. When the house was restored in the twentieth century, coloured glass from a demolished church was placed in the windows of the door. The clear glass in the transom window (above the door) is original, with more church glass placed behind it. When viewed from the narrow hallway inside, the coloured glass is very attractive. At the top of the windows in the door are wooden half-sunburst patterns. The wood trim on the second-floor gables is not original, but is a faithful copy. The front doors were purchased at an auction and are authentic indicators of the era in which the dwelling was constructed.

Above the first-floor gable, on the edge of the roof, is the original decorative wrought-iron trim, and the same material was employed for the attractive fence surrounding the front of the house. However, the fence was purchased in Dashwood, Ontario (London-Stratford area). Cast in the 1880s, it came from a grave in a churchyard. It is worth examining the unusual latch on the gate.

The door opens to a hallway where there are ornate decorations in the wood trim. The parlour is to the left of the hallway. The floors are pine, but in the hallway, the original flooring has been replaced with old oak. At the rear is a large kitchen, which possesses a rolled tin ceiling. The ceiling was not in the house when it was constructed but is typical of ceiling coverings that were in homes and shops in this era.

Houses with mansard roofs, 17 and 15 Draper Street.

21 Draper Street, on March 7, 1938, shortly before it was demolished. A parkette is now located on the site..

City of Toronto Archives, Series 372, Sub-series 33, Item 318

15 Draper Street, East Side

Built in 1881, this dwelling is one of a pair of Second Empire homes with mansard roofs. Its first occupant was Mrs. W. D. Jarvis (widow). The windows in the door and transom contain pleasing blue-green coloured glass, which creates a leaf pattern. These are not original but were added in later years. However, they are attractive and complement the home.

13 Draper Street, East Side

Built in 1881, after its construction was completed, this house remained unsold for two years. Its first owner was Mrs. M. A. Boyd, widow of Robert Boyd. The home is similar to others on the street, except that there are words inscribed on the glass of the transom window above the door. Though some letters are missing, the message remains legible. It advertises that the resident was an importer of ladies' fashions from Europe. During the summer months, the present owner (as of 2009) maintained a small garden and a charming water fountain.

Returning to Wellington Street West

The Portland Centre, 495–517 Wellington Street West
Southeast corner of Portland Street and Wellington Street West

In 1884, on this corner was the mansion of William A. Lee, a real estate and loan agent. It was one of the finest houses on the street. In 1906, the house was vacant and for sale. It was not purchased until 1912, when Copp Clark and Company, a publishing firm founded in 1909, bought the land.

The large 1884 house was demolished, and the architectural firm of Wickson and Gregg designed a red-brick factory and warehouse for the site. The name "Copp Clark" remains in evidence above the west door, and the old wooden sign survives on the west wall facing Portland Street. The factory structure possesses stylized stone designs on its simple façade. Inside the doorway (below the Copp Clark sign), there is a marble staircase, surrounded by decorative marble and wood trim, with an impressive pair of oak doors.

In 1928, another building was added, designed by the same architects as the original structure, although its façade was less ornate. The two factories were eventually connected, and the elevators of the complex were placed within this structure. The western building today is the offices of a film production company, and the eastern building has multiple tenants.

520 Wellington Street West, northeast corner of Portland and Wellington.

520 Wellington Street West

The semi-detached house on the northeast corner of Wellington and Portland, was constructed in 1891 and occupied the following year by Mrs. Sarah Scofield, who remained in the residence until 1897. In 1908, James McCartney, a foreman at the Canadian Pacific Railway, was the owner. Patrizi Gaetano was the resident who lived in the dwelling the longest. He bought the house in 1931 and remained there until 1947.

The slate tiles of the three-storey, red-brick house have not survived, but the asphalt replacements are arranged in the fish-scale pattern similar to the original tiles. It shared a chimney with its neighbour to the east, in an era when large fireplaces were essential to heat the rooms. There are small, decorative leaded windows above the large rectangular windows on the second floor. The wood cornice along the edge of the roof has simple, straight lines.

The original doorway has survived. The house now has the postal address 520A. It can be viewed from the west side of the property. The front of the home is obscured by a red-brick extension added to the front of the building in 1949 by George Fomby, who opened a shop named Portland Grocery. Unfortunately, it destroyed the symmetrical design of the two houses.

The year Portland Grocery Store commenced, the street was evolving from a residential neighbourhood into a commercial district. However, sufficient families remained to justify the investment, as it was a decade when every community needed a corner store. Mr. Fomby was one of the first merchants to install a telephone to permit customers to place orders and have them delivered. The telephone number was TR (Trinity) 0614. The store was also very popular with children, as it sold penny candy. At the front of the shop was a door, but the one that remains today is unlikely the original. The large window of the old shop is in evidence, but it has been modernized. It is likely that Portland Groceries extended back and occupied a good-sized portion of the ground-floor level of the house.

Victoria Memorial Square, October 14, 1913.
City of Toronto Archives, Series 372, Sub-Series 52, Item 192

Victoria Memorial Square

The green space at the west end of Wellington Street West.

The Garrison Burying Ground

The small open space known as Victoria Square was larger in the nineteenth century than it is today. The boundaries of the burial ground within the square formed a rectangle, with the corners pointing to the four cardinal points of the compass. This was unusual, as it was the custom of the day to align plots parallel to the grid. Almost all streets were also planned according to the gridlines. The reason for the unusual configuration of the cemetery is unknown. At that time, the only other site in the community that was positioned in a similar manner was "Belle Vue," the home of the Denison Family, located in Denison Square in the present-day Kensington Market area.

When completed in 1794, the cemetery was entirely surrounded by dense forest. The trees were cut down by Simcoe's troops. Those existing in the square were planted in the twentieth century. In the 1830s, when the land was surveyed and the streets were laid out, the small square was bounded on the north by Stewart Street, the south by Niagara Street, the east by Portland Street, and the west by Bathurst Street. During the years ahead, houses were erected on its western section (on Bathurst Street), reducing the size of the square. Wellington Place ended at the east side of the cemetery. Eventually a street named Douro was cut through the square. This new street, as well as Wellington Place, were eventually combined and renamed Wellington Street West, as it is today.

Governor Simcoe's daughter Katherine, who was only fifteen months of age when she died, was the first interment in the cemetery. During the following years, many more were buried, including at least one of the soldiers who perished defending York in the American invasion of 1813. During the War of 1812, York was a medical centre where they brought those who had been injured in battles on the Niagara frontier. Reverent John Strachan reported that in 1813 he officiated at the funerals for six to eight men a day.

It is estimated that from the time of its inception in 1794 until the final interment in 1863, about four hundred bodies were placed within the grounds. In the years ahead, citizens of the town were also buried here, though after 1807 many were placed in the churchyard of St. James, on King Street East. With the closing of the First Garrison Burying Ground, another cemetery was created to the northwest of Fort York, on Dufferin Street, near the present-day Canadian National Exhibition grounds.

It is worth mentioning a few of those who were buried here in the old Garrison Cemetery, now Victoria Memorial Square. Most of the names that follow were identified by John Ross Robertson during visits to the cemetery in the 1870s. They were recorded in his book *Landmarks of Toronto,* Volume 1, (Mika Publishing, Belleville, 1987). As of 2009, the stones were no longer in evidence. They will likely be included when the park's restoration has been completed.

- Christopher Robinson, father of John Ross Robertson, died 1798.
- Benjamin Hallowell, a relative of Chief Justice Elmsley, died Thursday, March 28, 1799, age 75.

- John Edward Sharps, infant son of J. E. and M. Sharps, died at 9 months on August 8, 1813.
- Captain McNeal killed in the Battle of York, 1813, during the American invasion of Toronto.
- Charlotte, wife of John Armitage, died April 8, 1819.
- John Saumariez Colbourne, died May 1, 1826, three-year-old son of Sir John Colbourne.
- Mackay John Scobie, died August 26, 1834, age 18, and his brother Kenneth Scobie, age 25, died in 1834. Their father was Captain John Scobie of the 93rd Highlanders.
- Margaret Ryan, wife of William Ryan of the Canadian Rifles, died 1835.
- Lieutenant Zachariah Mudge, private secretary to Sir John Colbourne (Lord Seaton), committed suicide by placing a gun to his chest. He died at age 31 on June 10, 1831.
- Barbara Mary, daughter of Reverend J. Hudson, died July 17, 1831.
- Archibald Currie of Glasgow, Scotland. Robertson states that the stone was too corroded to decipher any other details.

Final burial in the Garrison Cemetery was Private James McQuarrick in 1863.

An interesting notation claims that Captain Battersby, a British soldier, when ordered back to Britain following the War of 1812, shot his two horses and buried them in the cemetery, rather than part with them by selling them to someone else. Thankfully, he did not plan a similar fate for the friends he left behind in tiny York.

Veterans' Monument in the Centre of the Square

The ceremony to unveil the memorial was held on July 1, 1902, as a part of the Dominion Day (Canada Day) celebrations. Veterans of the British Army and Navy placed the monument in the square. It honours the memory of those who lost their lives defending Upper Canada during the War of 1812 (1812–1815). The regiments that served in the conflict and the names of the battlefields are listed on plaques attached to the monument.

In 1906 a sculpture of the torso of a veteran was added to its crown. The balding soldier appears to be glancing upward, a weary expression on his face. He is attired in a military uniform displaying war medals, and in his right hand is his hat. His left arm has no hand, perhaps a casualty of battle. Katherine Hale, in her book *Toronto, Romance of a Great City*, (Cassell and Company, Toronto, 1956), states, "The soldier has an unusual face—strong, rapt and dedicated."

The statue was created by Walter Allward, who also cast the figures at the south base of the Boer War Memorial at University Avenue and Queen Street West. In addition, Allward designed the Canadian war memorial on the Douri plain at Vimy Ridge.

The stone base of the monument in Victoria Memorial Square is similar in design to the one at Queenston Heights to commemorate the deeds of Laura Secord, a heroine of the War of 1812.

The monument in Victoria Memorial Square, c. 1906.
City of Toronto Archives, Fonds 1257, File 257, Item 188

There is an historic plaque on the north side of the square, near Wellington Street West, commemorating the demolished Anglican Church of St. John the Evangelist, also known as St. John's or simply the Garrison

Church. St. James on King Street East was two miles to the east of Fort York. In the early days of Toronto, the roads were impossibly muddy in spring, and in winter, often impassable with snow. Therefore, travelling to services at St. James was a hardship for the troops when the weather was inclement.

As a result, funds were raised, and to the north of the cemetery, the wood-framed church of St. John's was erected in 1858, with a capacity of five hundred. It was replaced in 1893 with a more permanent structure of brick. Eden Smith designed the new church in the early English Gothic style, with a simple rectangular tower. It was officially consecrated by Archbishop William Hay. A school room was also constructed on the west side of the church, facing Stewart Street.

After the British troops departed from Canada and the city expanded westward, the number of families worshipping at St. John's slowly diminished. The church was deconsecrated in 1963 and demolished. The schoolhouse survived until the summer of 2003, when it was torn down to allow a condominium to be constructed. This destruction of history was accomplished without any public notice or input. Nothing appeared in any of the newspapers, as if the old building had been completely unworthy of attention. Another part of the city's heritage disappeared forever.

The Simcoes in Toronto

The Simcoe family was closely linked to the history of Victoria Memorial Square. After the Simcoes arrived in Toronto and their supplies were taken ashore, the troops erected their tents on a small clearing of land, close to the lake and to the east of a stream that became known as Garrison Creek. In the days ahead, the Queens Rangers, of which there were about two hundred, set to work clearing the land of trees. The few settlers who already resided in Toronto were located in simple dwellings of log construction, at the eastern end of the harbour.

During the summer of 1793, plans were made to create the new capital. Work began on the construction of Yonge Street as far north as Lake Simcoe, which was named after John Graves Simcoe's father. The road was distant from the American border and, therefore, provided a safe route to the west for the fur trade, connecting through the Severn River to Georgian Bay.

In June, Deputy-Surveyor Alexander Aitkin drew up plans for the small settlement. At the eastern end of the harbour, not far west of the Don River, he laid out ten blocks. Each block was 264 by 264 feet, surrounded by 66 feet of space to allow for the streets. In total, it consisted of about sixteen acres. Before the Queen's Rangers cleared the trees, the community was surveyed and they decided which areas would be reserved for specific purposes. During the years ahead, the drawings disappeared, but in 1900, a researcher found them in London in the Public Records Office on Chancery Lane.

On August 27, 1793, when the name of the capital was changed from Toronto to York, the town contained about twelve houses, mostly of roughly hewn logs. The following year tragedy struck the Simcoes when Katherine, their fifteen-month-old daughter, developed a sudden chill and died. There was no church, and thus no parish records were available in which to record her name. However, in England, on receiving the news of the child's death, Mrs. Hunt entered it in the parish records of Dunswell, Devon.

Historical records remain today that detail funerary practices of the time. They allow us to imagine the scene in the small Garrison Cemetery in 1794. A small coffin of an appropriate size would have been crafted by a carpenter of the Queen's Rangers. It was likely of pine or basswood, and it was custom to stain it with lampblack. Because there was no undertaker in York to prepare the body, it was necessary to bury little Katherine within twenty-four hours of her demise. With no church available in which to hold a service, the day after Katherine's passing, her hastily prepared coffin was placed on the shoulders of several soldiers and carried to the cemetery, where a simple ceremony was held beside the open grave.

Elizabeth would have worn a black dress, a standard part of every woman's wardrobe. Civilian men would be attired in black, and the soldiers would have placed black armbands on the sleeves of their green uniforms. The same year that Katherine Simcoe passed away, news reached York that Queen Marie Antoinette had been executed. Mrs. Simcoe recorded that in the evening everyone at York dressed in black, even the children. All public events were cancelled, as well as dances and dinner parties.

The following year, a marble tombstone arrived from Honiton (East Devon), but it is not known what happened to it. A resident of Toronto searched the cemetery in 1850 and reported that it had disappeared without a trace. As a result, today we do not know where the final resting place of Katherine Simcoe is located within Victoria Square.

In July of 1795, Simcoe and his family sailed for England. Although his appointment as lieutenant-governor did not end until 1798, he spent the last three years of his commission in Britain. He and Elizabeth hoped that they would be able to return to Upper Canada, but fate conspired against them. They never set foot in York or the Garrison Cemetery again.

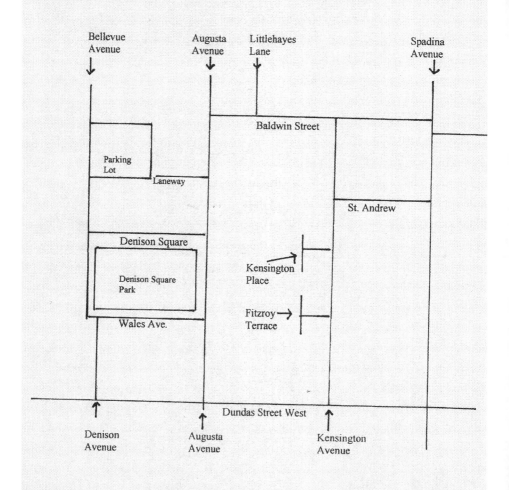

The Kensington Market District

Chapter Four:

The Kensington Market

Baldwin Street in the Kensington Market, July afternoon in 2009.

The Kensington Market is located west of Spadina Avenue, south of College Street, bounded on the south by Dundas Street and on the west by Bellevue Avenue.

This glimpse into the Kensington Market was completed during the summer of 2009 and reflects the way it existed at that time. Because the area is ever changing, it is impossible to predict how long the information will remain accurate. The history will not change, but the owners of the buildings may demolish or alter them to the degree that they will no longer be recognizable. The book, *Kensington* (Jane Cochrane, with photographs by Vincenzo Pietropaolo, Boston Mills Press, 2000) was an excellent source of background information on the market, and I am grateful for the insights it provided.

Torontonians do not usually refer to the Kensington Market as a "village." The dictionary defines a village as "a group of homes that is larger than a hamlet and smaller than a town." However, as anyone who has experienced the villages of Ontario can verify, a village is much more than this. Villages have boundaries, alerting travelers when they have arrived within its precincts and when they have departed. Every village has a different character and an atmosphere that throughout the decades the villagers have created.

This is true of "Kensington." The residents tend to be community oriented, many of them maintaining a keen sense of neighbourhood. Although they have values that they hold in common, they also have a true sense of individualism. Many of the residents are environmentalists, enjoy health foods, and strongly support recycling. As well, many ethnic groups reside within the area.

Others are aging hippies, leftover flower children, and leather types. Some follow lifestyles that defy categorization. Yet there are also those whose lifestyle is indistinguishable from other residents of the city. It is evident that a few are restoring their homes to capture the appearance of the nineteenth century, rather than simply renovating, as they have a keen interest in the history of the area. The Market has a few colourful eccentrics who are well accepted and considered an integral part of the scene.

Other cities in the world have districts within their boundaries that are similar to Kensington, forming small enclaves that maintain their unique character despite the passage of time. They too share common characteristics, but no two are ever alike. Although many have historic homes and quaint shops, nowhere is there another Kensington.

It is "one of a kind"—a chaotic collage of diversity.

Richard Florida, in his book *The Rise of the Creative Class,* discusses places where the residents are seeking an environment that is open to differences, where highly creative people are welcomed, regardless of ethnic background, income, creed, or sexual orientation. They prefer locations where their multiplicity is accepted, where odd personal habits or extreme styles of dress are not only welcomed, but also celebrated.

Unusual marital arrangements and varied partnership relations fail to attract any attention.

Kensington is such a place, and is truly "a village within."

Kensington: In the Beginning

In the 1790s, the site where Kensington Market now exists was contained within two of the land grants that they referred to as "park lots." Alexander Grant owned one of them, and the other was in the possession of Major E. B. Littlehayes. The name Littlehayes survives to this day in the name of a small laneway that extends north from Baldwin Street, east of Augusta Avenue.

The Denison Family

The story of today's Kensington Market is entwined with the history of the Denison Family. In the early days of the nineteenth century, when they constructed their home, which they named Belle Vue, they were the only family living in the area. During those decades, forests covered the land, among which a few open meadows dotted the landscape and where wild flowers grew in abundance each summer.

The family had its roots in Britain. Captain John Denison was born in 1755 in Headon, Yorkshire, England. At twenty-seven years of age he married seventeen-year-old Sophia Taylor of Dovercourt, in Essex. The young bride had attended school with Elizabeth Russell, the sister of Peter Russell. John Denison was a miller and malt master by trade, but enlisted in the British Army to fight in the American Revolutionary War. While serving in the military, Denison became acquainted with Peter Russell, the husband of his wife's friend.

When the conflict ended, they were close friends. In 1792, John Denison was persuaded by Peter Russell to immigrate to Upper Canada (Ontario). Denison had three young sons—George Taylor, Thomas John, and Charles. The Denison family settled in Kingston and lived in a rented mill. Within a year, Denison realized that his chances of success in Kingston were limited, as there was an insufficient supply of barley to support his malting business.

In the summer of 1793, Denison travelled to Niagara-on-the-Lake and informed his friend Peter Russell that due to his lack of prospects, he intended to return to England. Governor Simcoe learned of Denison's problems and invited him to dine at Navy Hall, beside the Niagara River. During the course of the dinner, Simcoe suggested that Denison move to Toronto, as Simcoe intended to rename it "Dublin." John Denison replied that as a loyal Englishman he could never reside in a town with an Irish name. He was a man who was fiercely loyal to the British Empire, the Church of England, and the Tory Party, the political wing of the church.

According to Denison, as a result of this conversation, Simcoe changed his mind and promised to bestow the name York on the new capital. This version of the naming of York was never recorded in the history books, but in the years ahead, Denison repeated it many times to his friends and dinner guests. It became part of his personal lore.

Dublin was the name first given to the Township of York, which eventually became the City of York, now included within the boundaries of the City of Toronto.

The Denisons in Colonial York

When the Denisons arrived in York, they were granted land that they considered remote from the provincial capital. John Denison received title to a thousand acres of land near the present-day town of Weston, on the east bank of the Humber River. He built a home and called the estate Black Creek Farm, the name surviving to this day in Black Creek Boulevard, Black Creek Pioneer Village, and the small stream Black Creek, which empties into the Humber River a short distance south of Eglinton Avenue. (Conrad Black was not a part of this name giving, although a few newspapers have freely given him a few names of their own.)

Because there was very little entertainment in this isolated location, three more children were born to the family while they resided at Black Creek Farm—John, Elizabeth (who died in infancy), and Elizabeth Sophia (named after her godmother, Elizabeth Russell). The family cemetery was established at Black Creek Farm, and tiny Elizabeth was buried within its grounds, high on the cliffs above the Humber River. The cemetery remains on the site today.

In 1796, John Denison, disenchanted with living in a remote location far from the town, relocated his family to York. For a few months they lived in Governor Simcoe's former residence, Castle Frank, on a hill overlooking the Don River. Peter Russell was able to allow him to reside in Castle Frank as when Simcoe had returned to England, he had left the dwelling in his care.

Peter Russell was now the receiver general of Upper Canada, a very important position within the administration of the colony. In York, he owned park lot 14, located in the Queen/Spadina area. He had named his estate Petersfield.

Peter Street, in downtown Toronto, received its name because it formed the roadway that led to Petersfield. Russell Hill Road was also named in his honour. In 1796, Russell employed Denison as his estate manager, and provided a home for him on the site.

When the War of 1812 was declared, John Denison served as captain of the Third York Militia. This was a very unusual war, as it was one of the few conflicts in which both sides claimed victory. The American invasion of York, in 1813, had an enormous impact on the young colony. When the war ended, Denison had saved sufficient funds to purchase park lot 25 from David Burns, an army surgeon. The total cost was two hundred pounds. This was in the area of present-day Queen and Ossington. He built a family home and named it Brookfield. Today, Brookfield Avenue is a street in the Queen-Ossington area. Denison vacated Brookfield in the years after they built the insane asylum, as it was referred to in those days, on the south side of Queen Street. Today, they are redeveloping the grounds of the hospital to make it more inclusive of its surroundings. When completed, it will resemble another village within the city.

Most of the old brick wall that surrounds the premises, has survived into the modern era. What a wonderful location it could be for an "art wall." The idea has been employed successfully for decades in Jackson Square, in New Orleans. In this city, wrought-iron fencing creates the wall. Each day, artists display their paintings and crafts to potential buyers. It is a lively, colourful scene, much loved by the city's residents and tourists alike.

In Toronto, the brick wall of the asylum has similar potential. Granted, it would be seasonal and likely only on weekends. However, what a wonderful location for aspiring and established artists to hang their paintings. The mature trees of the grounds would shade the participants from the hot, summer sun. A city can never have too many locales such as these.

The Denison Family in the Kensington Area

George Taylor Denison, oldest son of John Denison, was nine years old when he arrived in Canada with his father. In 1806, at twenty-seven years of age, he married Esther Borden Lippincott, whose father owned three thousand acres in the Richmond Street area of York. Like his father, George Denison had also served in the War of 1812. It had been his responsibility to supervise the construction of the road from the town to Lambton Mills on the banks of the Humber River. It became the Dundas Street of today.

Similar to his father, after the war George Denison purchased land. In 1815, he bought lot number 17 from Alexander Grant, and park lot 18 from Major E. B. Littlehayes. These properties were bounded by the modern-day streets of Spadina, Dundas Street West, Lippincott, and Bloor. The modern-day Kensington Market is within these boundaries.

Belle Vue

The same year that George Denison acquired the land, he commenced construction of a home on the property and named it Belle Vue. It was located on the land that today is the site of the Kiever Synagogue, at the northwest corner of Bellevue Square Park. When he built his new home, he was forty-two years of age. He ordered that the land in front of Belle Vue be cleared to create an open square—a promenade in which to stroll. It also created an impressive setting for the home, amid the surrounding forests. Because Denison was a colonel in the militia, the square was used occasionally to drill troops or stage a military parade. The Denison family eventually donated the square to the city, and today it exists as Bellevue Square Park. It is in the heart of the modern-day Kensington Market and is the scene of many community events.

The Denison Family at Belle Vue

George Taylor Denison and Esther (nee Lippincott) raised three children in Belle Vue—Richard Lippincott (born 1814), George Taylor II (born 1816), and Robert Brittain (born 1821). The youngest son, Robert, inherited Belle Vue when his father died in 1853. Shortly after he gained title to the property, he hired J. Stoughton Dennis to subdivide the estate into individual lots suitable for erecting homes. This had become necessary as he needed funds to pay the daily living expenses at Belle Vue.

If he were to find purchasers for the building lots, it was essential that they carve streets out of the wilderness to allow public access to the sites. The streets were named after places in England, such as Oxford, Cambridge (now Nassau), and Wales. Other names were derived from the Denison family. In the years ahead, Robert Denison was influential in the life of the city. He served in the militia and fought against the Fenians when they raided Canada in the 1860s. He donated the land and funds to erect the Anglican Church of St. Stephen in the Fields, which remains in existence today at the southeast corner of Bellevue Avenue and College Street. He also served for many years on the city council, as the alderman for St. Patrick's Ward.

Robert sold Belle Vue in 1889 and they demolished the home in 1890. When he died in 1900, virtually no land from the original park lot remained in his possession, other than the small piece of property that his home occupied.

The Denison Family's Legacy in Present-day Toronto

Robert's older brother, Richard Lippincott Denison, married Susan Hepbourne. Their home, Dover Court, was built in 1839 and named after his mother's ancestral home in Essex. At that time it was a rural setting amid the forest, surrounded with floral gardens and orchards. Robert's other brother, George Taylor Denison II, married Mary Anne Dewson, and their home was named Rush Holme, near present-day Dovercourt and College. They raised eight sons and one daughter on the estate.

The names and homes of these members of the Denison family are reflected in the street names of the downtown area of Toronto—Lippincott, Hepbourne, Dewson, Rusholme, and Dovercourt, all of which survive to this day.

Visiting the Kensington Market

This study begins at Bellevue Square Park, bounded by Augusta Avenue on the east and Bellevue Avenue on the west. Today, the square contains a statue to Al Waxman, the "King of Kensington" of television fame. Waxman was born at 74 Wales Avenue, a short distance from the square. The family rented two rooms on the second floor from Mr. and Mrs. Greenbaum. Later, the Waxmans moved to 414A Spadina Avenue (near Nassau St.).

The children's wading pool in Bellevue Square Park is well used in summer. Surrounding the square are many nineteenth-century homes. Most have their original doors, though sometimes they are covered with modern storm doors.

Long gone are the days when this area was a wilderness forest. However, early-day photographs of the square depict trees that were mature in 1914—an old sycamore and a maple on the east of side of the square, and on the south side, a silver maple and another sycamore. It is possible that these are survivors from the early 1800s.

In 1889, Bellevue Square Park was assessed by the city as having a value of $10,395. This was determined on the basis that it was of five building lots, each having a dimension of 297 feet by 150 feet, each lot with a value of $2079.

When the Denisons resided in Belle Vue, there were fewer trees in the square than today, as the land had been cleared to provide an unobstructed view southward, down Denison Avenue. The pine trees that now occupy the square were planted in the final decades of the twentieth century. The maples that mark the western boundary of the square are likely twenty or thirty years old. In the photographs of 1913, a white stone fountain was evident in the northeast quadrant. There were walkways that criss-crossed the square from each corner.

**Bellevue Square on October 14, 1913, with a
fountain in the middle of the square.**

City of Toronto Archives, Fonds 372, Sub-series 52, Item 197

Sarah Bayne (nee Gordon), who lived on Wales Avenue, standing beside the fountain in Bellevue Square, c. 1930. It is a different fountain than the one that appears in the 1914 photograph. The Kiever Synagogue is visible in the background, as well as the houses on the west side of the square, on Bellevue Avenue.

Photo courtesy of Colby Bayne, from his personal collection.

There were four different eras in the life of the Kensington Market. The time periods overlap as the transition from one phase to another was always gradual.

1. The Victorian and Edwardian Era (c.1860–c.1910)
2. The Jewish Market (c.1900–c.1960)
3. The Multicultural Market (c.1950–today)
4. The hip, the cool, and the retro (c.1990–?)

The Victorian Era in Kensington

Wales Avenue

This street, formerly known as Bellevue Place, is the southern boundary of Bellevue Square Park.

The home of James R. Peterkin at 29 Wales Avenue.

29 Wales Avenue
Home on the southwest corner of Bellevue Square Park

Although the interior of this impressive house is relatively quiet today, when its original owner resided there, it was a lively, bustling home. In the

1880s, seven children lived within its walls. Parental discipline was strict in this era, however, as ever, children discovered ways to create fun and break a few rules, while hoping to receive lenient punishments.

It is likely that they scattered toys on the floors of the upper hallways, and occasionally their parents found them on the steps of the stairs. After the gas lamps were extinguished for the night, much whispering and quiet giggling was invariably heard in the children's bedrooms. Occasionally, an older child might have sneaked into a younger sibling's room to inflict a harmless prank.

If the walls of this house were able to speak, they would perhaps reveal secrets and stories that we would find amusing today. Perhaps a few indiscretions on the part of the parents would be included in the telling.

When James R. Peterkin purchased the empty building lot, he had already acquired a considerable income. In 1865, when he was only twenty-one, he had established a lumber mill and yard at 145 Bay Street. Newspaper advertisements for his lumber yard stated, "Builder, cabinet maker, turnings kept constantly on hand, all kind of plain and fancy mouldings, floor sheeting, re-sawing, scroll and band sawing, shaping and Daniel's planing, etc."

In the ensuing years, Peterkin prospered, and he built his first home on this site at 29 Wales Avenue. It was a one-storey dwelling in the Ontario cottage style, with large verandas wrapped around the north and east sides. In 1884, having obtained further success in his business, he decided to demolish his first home and construct a larger dwelling for his young family, as he and his wife had seven children. This is the home that you see before you today. He lived here until 1910. Five years after it was built, the home had a value of $3500, and the land was worth $3325.

The three-storey house is red brick, likely from Don Valley Brickyard. Five horizontal rows of yellow bricks decorate the façade, and draw attention to the home's design, which reflects the affluence of its builder. The third floor, with its dormer window, is hidden in summer by the large tree at the front of the house. The ornate trim around the porch displays the quality of the wood products that Peterkin's company produced. The intricate designs in the pediment (triangle) above the porch were cut with a scroll saw. The porch-supports (pillars) display a high degree of carpentry skill.

The outer and inner doors appear to be originals, as is the attractive transom window over the outside front door. It has ornate hinges, but the designs are visible only when the door is open. When Peterkin welcomed visitors to the home, the fancy hinges were exposed. This attention to detail illustrates the pride he expressed in his dwelling.

On either side of the inside door there are sidelight windows. They contain frosted glass, but the pattern in the panes is clear glass, depicting a floral design containing roses and shamrocks. In the entrance hall, there is an ornately carved post at the bottom of the stairs that leads to the second floor. The wood mouldings on either side of the stairs are fourteen inches high. The dwelling is an excellent example of a prosperous merchant's home of the late-Victorian period.

In the twentieth century, Dan Heaps resided here. He was an Anglican minister and was at one time the alderman for Ward Six. He was also an MPP for the New Democratic Party. He sold the house for a nominal sum to a charitable group.

Note:

The row of houses that are now examined are on the South side of Wales Avenue, between Denison Avenue (on the west) and Augusta Avenue (on the east).

These row houses were built by R. S. Dinnick between the years 1889 and 1890. The lots varied in value from $391 to $571, and so the houses also differed in price. The lowest selling price was $1500, and the highest was $2000. As a result, the final selling prices of the land and houses ranged from $1896 to $2577.

21 Wales Avenue

Constructed in 1890, the dwelling at number 21 is an excellent example of the type of row houses built in Toronto during the final decades of the nineteenth century. The first occupant at 21 Wales was Henry (Harry) Hutchinson, who rented it from the builder. The year he moved into the house, it was valued at $1925. Hutchinson was employed by W. J. Sommerville and Company at 575 Queen Street West, just two doors from Portland Avenue. The company sold quality dry goods, carpets, oilcloth, and rugs.

Mr. Hutchinson was not particularly prosperous, but he possessed better financial means than many of the working-class people in Toronto. He had rented a new house in a newly developed residential area, within walking distance of the downtown and close to the many shops on Queen Street West.

Though he was only an employee at W. J. Summerville and Company, he was likely in management or was in charge of a department, as his wages were sufficient to allow him to rent this excellent property. Except in the most severe weather, his walk to work was less than fifteen minutes. People he passed along the way were customers, and invariably he met a few neighbours, some of whom likely envied his relative success. Mr. Hutchinson was able to purchase many of the items to furnish his home with his employee discount, adding to his already good fortune. Five years later, he departed from 21 Wales Avenue. He likely purchased a home of his own, perhaps a more modest dwelling.

In 1895, James P. Paterson occupied the house. He was a foreman at A. A. Allan and Company, a wholesale furrier located at 511 Bay Street. In 1903, George W. Peavey, owner of the Canadian Wine Company at 885 Queen Street West, occupied the house.

Though streetcars, originally pulled by horses, had appeared on the main streets of Toronto by the middle of the nineteenth century, most considered them too expensive to ride on a daily basis. As a result, the majority resided where it was possible to walk to work. Number 21 Wales was indeed an excellent location. The brickwork of number 21 has been cleaned, and the home appears much as it did when it was first constructed. There are unpretentious brick patterns above the door, as well as under the second-storey windows. The home possesses balanced proportions, with straight architectural lines.

Because the home was exposed to the bitter north winds during the long Canadian winters, a set of outer doors was necessary to protect the interior. In warm weather, the doors were folded back against the walls inside the archway. There is red glass in the transom window above the inner door. Both the inner and the outer doors are original. The home shares a chimney with the adjoining house. The chimney pot, inserted in the chimney, reduced the risk of sparks igniting the roof.

The dwelling contains five bedrooms—three on the second floor and two on the third level. When visitors step into the front hallway, they find the staircase to the second floor immediately on their right. It contains a hand-carved railing with a handsome post at the bottom. Throughout the home, there is a great deal of wood trim, with fourteen-inch baseboard moulding. The parlour is on the left side of the front hallway, and sliding doors separate it from the kitchen. The kitchen ceiling is patterned rolled tin, which was very popular in the late-Victorian and Edwardian years. As late as the early 1920s, some homes continued to employ this type of ceiling

The kitchen cupboards occupy the entire east wall, and the moulding around the top of the kitchen contains the Greek egg-and-dart pattern. This design was popular to decorate public buildings in classical times and was revived in the eighteenth century for both public and domestic use. It is possible to find this design in moulding showrooms to this very day.

The present owner purchased the house in 2001 and has since restored the interior. The south wall of the kitchen now has floor-to-ceiling glass doors, which open on a small patio with a wooden deck. With a southern exposure, it has plenty of winter sunlight, and when the summer sun is high in the sky, it is shaded from the afternoon heat.

19 Wales Avenue

Also built in 1890, this home possesses the original slate rock shingles. A close examination of the tiles on the gable roof reveals that in a small section they employed the "variegated" pattern. It too has inner and outer doors in the entranceway, but the outside door and transom window above it are modern. A basement window has been altered to provide an entrance door to the cellar.

9 Wales Avenue

Built in 1890, this home was first occupied by Simon Foster, who earned his living as a grocer. He remained in the residence at 9 Wales Avenue for five years. In 1895, he relocated to 790 College Street, where he opened a grocery store that included a post office, and lived in the rooms above the store. The next occupant of #9 Wales was Percy P. Kerwin. In 1903, John M. Mains, who was an engineer, took possession.

Today the façade of this three-storey bay-and-gable home has been cleaned. The pediment at the top has been altered and the ornate trim removed. The pattern in the brickwork under the second-floor windows was created by simply alternating the position of the bricks.

7 Wales Avenue

This building's construction was completed in 1890, and in that year, Mrs. Mary Foster moved into the dwelling. She was the widow of Charles P. Foster, who, along with a business partner, owned Foster and Macabe, a store that specialized in "fancy goods." It was located at 51 Yonge Street. It was a modestly successful business, and with the income from her husband's estate, Mary was able to purchase this home.

As a widow with a modest income, life was sometimes harsh for her, as in this era there were no government programs to assist those suffering from financial hardships. It was likely that she lived a frugal lifestyle. In an era without refrigerators, she shopped sparingly each day, and similar to most people, did not allow any food to be wasted. Many a meal consisted of soup or stew, incorporating the previous night's leftovers.

However, despite her prudent ways, once a year we can imagine her ordering a new dress from a dressmaker on Queen Street West. The fabric for the dress was also likely bought on the same street. When she stood in the dressmaker's shop for her "fitting," she was aware that a widow's life was not easy but felt that a new dress helped relieve the pains of living without her husband.

Dwelling in a new row house also helped, as neighbours were close by. In these years, neighbours knew each other well and provided each other with emotional support in difficult times. They shared their joys, sorrows, and the occasional bit of gossip. Being a widow, it is likely that Mary had learned to keep her cards close to her chest. If she entertained housewives of the other row houses for afternoon tea, she would be cautious in her conversations. Loose lips had been the downfall of many a widow.

Gazing at Mary's home today, one sees much of the original trim in the steep-pitch gable roof, which contains a sunburst pattern. The chimney on the west side of the roof has been removed. The missing chimney would have been similar to the one on 9 Wales Avenue. This means that the fireplace that she enjoyed is no longer in use.

If only Mary could greet us at the door today and tell us "real" stories of her life within this interesting row house.

On the east side of Denison Square Park is Augusta Avenue

189 Augusta Avenue

When the house was built in 1873, Augusta Avenue commenced at Dundas Street and ended at College. Today the street extends from Richmond to College Streets. The postal numbers of the houses were changed when the street was extended to the south. Augusta Avenue had been formerly known as Grosvenor Street. It was changed to Augusta, as there was another Grosvenor Street in the St. John's Ward, near Yonge and Wellesley Streets.

On the left-hand (north) side of the house there is a carriageway entrance. Today it provides access to the garage at the rear of the home. In the early twentieth century, it possessed large doors, which were opened and closed to allow a horse and carriage to enter or depart. Because the owner of 189 owned a carriage, it is assumed that he was reasonably affluent. This was an era when most people saved money by walking to their destinations, riding the streetcars on special occasions.

Unfortunately, not much of the original house is visible, as the entire façade has been covered with white brick. A small gable in the roof, on the third floor, is the only feature of the nineteenth-century home that is in evidence today.

197 Augusta Avenue

Built in 1884, this house still possesses its original veranda. Oscar F. Dodge was the first resident. He was an agent with the Manufacturers' Life Insurance Company. A successful businessman, he was able to afford this large home, residing on a street where a few neighbours possessed a stable and a fine carriage. The spacious rooms with their high ceilings were ideal for entertaining friends, including prospective clients. On these occasions, they likely completed more than a few business transactions.

In the 1880s, when people strolled past this house on a winter evening, the soft glow of the gaslights was visible through the large windows, hinting at the cozy scene within. Living in such a fine house was indeed pleasant, and the neighbours considered Oscar F. Dodge to be a fortunate man.

Today, examining the house, we are able to see dentils in the trim under the roof of the porch. The square-shaped wooden porch-supports (pillars) are a domestic vernacular version of Doric. The brickwork surrounding the first-floor window forms a Roman arch, with bricks placed vertically to create the keystone. On the second-floor level there is a charming bay window, and beneath it, graceful lines curve downward. The structure is an excellent example of a late-Victorian semi-detached home.

The present owner is restoring the home to its original appearance. The blue front door is new, but the owner selected it because of its nineteenth-century design. Though the dwelling is narrow, the rooms are spacious, as the house extends back for a considerable distance. There are rooms on four levels, with the basement having a separate entrance. Decks have been built across the back of the home to provide extra living space during the summer months.

The house is supported by large red sandstone blocks, similar to those employed at Toronto's Old City Hall. On the first floor, a sandstone block has been placed under the window, and another above the basement window.

The North Side of Denison Square Park

Prior to the 1880s, this street on the north side of Denison Square Park lacked an official name. Residents simply referred to their homes as being located on Denison Square. In the 1880s, the name "Bellevue Square" was given to the street. This was later changed to "Denison Square," the name it has retained to this day.

In 1885, the only residence on the north side of Bellevue Square Park was Belle Vue, the home of Robert Denison. His occupation was listed as "gentleman." However, by the following year, there were two unfinished homes among the vacant lots, and the home of John Murray at number 30 had been completed. The next year there were ten homes, and the postal numbering of the residences was revised. In the modern era, five homes on the north side of Denison Square were demolished to construct the Sasmart Store.

18 Denison Square

This asymmetrical home was built in 1887. Its first occupant was Clement Denison, a wholesale clerk with Wyld Brock and Company. Located at the corner of Bay and Wellington, the company sold dry goods and woollens. Clement was a member of the wealthy Denison family. When he moved into the house, he was twenty-five years old. The deed to the property was placed in the name of his wife, Edith Denison. It was an unusual arrangement in that decade, and the reason is not known.

In 1899, John James resided in the house. He was a millwright by trade, designing and constructing mills. In 1903, John C. Beavis, an insurance agent, lived here.

This house is perhaps the most architecturally interesting home in the row. When this opinion was expressed to the present-day owners, they modestly agreed. It is a three-storey dwelling with a mansard roof. Built on a lot that was thirty-two feet by one hundred, the year the house was constructed, the land and residence were assessed at $1250. It has a terrace on the second floor and a balcony on the third floor. In the triangle, high in the pediment, a fragmented sunburst pattern creates a plain design.

On the first floor, the dwelling has a spacious parlour and an attractive dining room. These rooms have fourteen-foot ceilings and contain the original moulding. The kitchen is located within an extension built across the rear of the home, likely constructed a few years after the main building.

The large bay windows in the alley on the west side add considerable light to the interior, especially in the second-floor bedroom. The master bedroom at the front of the second floor has no fireplace. In winter, the radiated heat from the flue of the fireplace below warmed the room. When gas heating and lighting were added to the house, possibly in the 1920s, the gas pipes were fitted against the walls rather than being encased inside them. Many of the original gas fixtures remain to this day. The flooring is oak on the first- and second-floor levels, but the third floor, likely the servants' quarters, is pine.

The present owners have planted a front garden containing peonies, yarrow, phlox, roses, hosta, and lily of the valley. The rear garden is very pleasant, a small island of privacy amid the hustle and bustle of the busy Kensington Market. Both gardens are reminders of Victorian times.

20 Denison Square

This is the only detached house in the row. Constructed in 1887, its first owner was Edward Callis, a grocer by trade. He was the only person on the street to build a brick shed in the garden at the rear of his property. The shed remains in existence today.

In 1889 the property at 20 Denison Square was valued at $960, and the house and shed at $450. An interesting pattern in the brickwork is evident under the upper windows. There is a Romanesque archway at the top of the doorway, and another one above the window on the first floor. Though the arches resemble cut stone, they are formed cement and are painted grey. There is an attractive patterned design in the wooden pediment in the peak.

In 1903, Daniel Casey lived at 20 Denison Square. He was a traveller with Elay Blain Company, wholesale grocers at 21–23 Front Street.

Note:

The homes from #20 Denison Square, west to Bellevue Avenue, were built on land that was once a part of the property surrounding the Denison home of Belle Vue.

The Kiever Synagogue

On the northwest corner of Denison Square and Bellevue Avenue is the Kiever Synagogue. It was constructed as a place of worship by Jewish immigrants who had fled religious persecution in the Ukraine. After arriving in Toronto, they commenced services in 1912 in "The Ward," a district to the east of University Avenue. By 1917, they relocated to the present-day site, on which there was a small house.

In 1927, they demolished the house and constructed the synagogue that you see before you today. Designed by Benjamin Swantz, it combines Romanesque and Byzantine architecture. It has two domed towers on the front and another at the northwest corner, each topped with a Star of David. No tower was built on the northeast corner of the building, as this corner was not visible from either of the streets that surround the synagogue. Four different styles of windows grace the façade, and although they vary in size, all have Romanesque arches over them.

There are separate doors for men and women, which lead to separate seating areas inside the sanctuary, which, in the traditional manner, faces Jerusalem.

The Kiever Synagogue, Kensington Market.

Belle Vue, the Home of the Denison Family

The Kiever Synagogue is on the site of Belle Vue, the home of Robert Taylor Denison. After Belle Vue was completed, a carriageway was cut to allow access from the square to Queen Street. The carriageway remains in existence today and is named Denison Avenue. It is possible to gaze from the spot where Belle Vue was located and view Queen Street to the south, but the forest of trees that lined the roadway has long since disappeared.

The Denison home was built in 1815 in the Loyalist Georgian style, with nine large shuttered windows across the front of the home. There were two spacious chimneys, one at either end of the dwelling. It was an era when large fireplaces were necessary to heat the rooms, because of their oversized dimensions and high ceilings. On either side of the doorway were sidelight windows that allowed light to enter the hallway. A small, ornate porch protected the doorway from the rain.

The house was covered with "roughcast," a mixture of cement and sand, and it was painted white. The roughcast gave protection from the weather and from fire. Belle Vue was positioned on the lot so that the four corners of the house were aligned with the points of the compass. It was the only building in York built in this manner, as the custom of the day was to situate homes parallel to the lot lines.

There were two out-buildings, one to the north of the house and the other to the west. Russell Creek flowed behind the house on its meandering course southeast toward Lake Ontario, a mile or two distant. The meandering creek with large willow trees growing along its banks, created a very pleasant rural picture. As the city developed, this stream was eventually buried to satisfy the demands of progress.

George Denison resided at Belle Vue until his death in 1853. The home was inherited by George Denison II, who immediately commenced subdividing the estate to acquire funds for his daily living expenses. Spacious lots were offered for a price of $350, but there were few buyers. He was forced to divide each of them into three smaller lots, which sold for $150 each. This is the reason why today, many of the houses are on narrow lots, well suited to row housing.

In 1889, when Denison was eighty years old, he decided to sell Belle Vue. At that time seven adults and one child resided in the house. In that year the land was assessed at a value of $3000, but the house was in a poor state of repairs and was valued at only $500. The out-buildings (likely a shed and carriage house) were also assessed at $500, the same amount as the house. The following year (1890) Belle Vue was demolished.

Bellevue Avenue, West Side of the Park

The Statue of Al Waxman

At the northwest quadrant of the park is a life-size statue of the actor Al Waxman, who became famous for his role as Larry King in the television program *The King of Kensington*. The CBC sitcom depicted the tribulations and joys of a convenience store operator who lived within the Kensington Market. The show was on the air from 1975 until 1980 and was very popular in its day.

Cast in bronze by the sculptor Ruth Abernathy, Waxman is shown wearing a suit and a turtleneck sweater. He stands between two park benches, one hand almost touching one of the benches. Waxman was born in 1935 in the Kensington area, and died in 2001. The names of his friends and supporters are carved into the back of one of the benches.

The statue of Al Waxman in Denison Square Park.

12 Bellevue Avenue

This house is across the street from the Al Waxman statue. Built on the west side of the park, it is one of six (three pairs) of single-family homes built in 1883. All six of the homes survive, although some of them have been greatly altered. On the front of one of them, they have built an addition, obscuring the nineteenth-century structure. At the time these houses were constructed, Canada's economy was recovering from an economic slump, and it was three years before one of them was sold.

In 1886, James Watt, who was an accountant at *The Globe* (later named *The Globe and Mail*) newspaper, rented number 12. The home is red brick with attractive yellow-brick designs to add detail to the façade. In the wood trim high in the peak there are small shamrock-like designs, and at the apex of the triangle there is a floral pattern.

Within a year, James Watt moved to a larger house at the corner of Bellevue and Wales, 2 Bellevue Avenue. David Adair now moved into number 12. He was thirty-two years old and employed as a salesman by W. A. Murray and Sons, located at 27 King Street East. This firm sold dry goods, including millinery, dressmaking, and clothing. In 1889, two years after David Adair moved in, the house and property were valued at $1600. At this time there were three adults and one child residing in the home. In 1903, the house was lived in by Mrs. Jessie Elliott, widow of Geo B. Elliott.

A few years ago, there were extensive renovations to the house. In the front bedroom, on the second floor, when the dry wall was removed, it was found that the upper-right-hand window had previously been a door. The door was restored and the upper veranda was rebuilt to reflect more of the original appearance of the house. The floor of the lower veranda is now cement and stone.

To accommodate the large tree at the front, the walkway leading to the house has a graceful curve. The bay windows of the first floor have storm windows, like those used in earlier days. The right-hand window contains small round "breathing holes" at the bottom, which can be opened by lifting the small wooden slat that covers them on the inside, allowing fresh air to enter the house on mild winter days.

The transom window over the door has a pleasing pattern of coloured glass. The design appears to have the stylized shape of a pineapple, the symbol of hospitality. The home indeed creates a pleasant and welcoming appearance.

20 Bellevue Avenue

They commenced construction of this home in 1874 and completed it a year later. When built, the land was worth $500 and the dwelling was assessed at $550, later increasing to $750. It possessed a slate roof, but today it is covered with blue shingles, and a large skylight has been added.

The trim on the peak is in good condition, and is dramatically painted in bold cobalt blue.

In 1875, Seymour J. Clark, a thirty-nine-year-old employee of the Grand Trunk Railway, moved in along with his wife and child. He rented the premises from the owner, Thomas Danson. During the next few years the house had a succession of residents.

There is a laneway at the left-hand (south) side, and there are three houses at the end of the lane. This is an example of the concept of a "house behind a house." There are four more examples of this in the Kensington area. The houses located at the end of the lane have the same postal number as the house on the street, but they have added the fraction ½. Number 16½ can be seen by peering down the laneway, which today is a private thoroughfare. A builder once lived in 14½ Bellevue Avenue (since demolished), and he will be mentioned later.

The tall smokestack and buildings of the Toronto (Western) Hospital can be seen to the west. In the previous century this was the park lot of the McDonald family, whose lands adjoined those of the Denison family. The western boundary of their property is today's Lippincott Street.

24 Bellevue Avenue

When the original owner moved into this house, the happy echo of children's voices dominated the domestic scene. It's likely that their father retreated often to the quiet of his den to escape the frantic activities of his children.

Built in 1874, this house is located on a lot that is 50 by 148 feet. The land had a value of $500 in that year, and the house was assessed at $700. It was purchased by Peter A. Wright, a "pattern maker." His business was quite successful, enabling him to afford such a fine home. At forty-seven years of age, he had seven children.

A red-brick house, the patterns on the façade are created by employing yellow bricks. During this period, many of the city's yellow bricks came from a brickyard in Yorkville (Yonge and Bloor area). Viewing the area today, with its chic boutiques and posh hotels, it is difficult to imagine the litter of a brickyard ever existing in the area.

The house at 24 Bellevue Avenue exhibits expert carpentry, visible in the detailed joinery work in the intricate designs in the peak, which at its apex has a sunburst pattern.

This bay-and-gable house possesses an impressive bay window that commences on the first floor and rises majestically to the roof. The style is indigenous to Toronto and allows maximum light to enter the interior. The coloured glass in the window above the door contains a circle, with various geometric shapes and a few graceful curved lines to add variety. The tops of the other windows have coloured glass as well. The front door appears to be original, and opens in two sections.

The present owner constructed a curved walkway approaching the house. There is a purple lilac bush on the lawn in front of the windows. If one visits the house on a spring day, when it is in bloom, the scent is heavy in the air. It is not difficult to imagine earlier days when the street was quieter, free from the fumes of automobiles, and quaint gardens were in greater abundance.

27 Bellevue Avenue, East Side

This detached house on the east side of the street was built in 1887 on land that had been a part of the grounds of the Denison home—Belle Vue. It was constructed by Thomas Crouch, a carpenter and builder, who had previously resided at the end of the laneway at 14½ Bellevue Avenue. He lived at 27 Bellevue from 1887 until 1889.

Relocating from the laneway to this fine house was a momentous occasion for Mr. Crouch. Being a carpenter and builder assisted him greatly and reduced his labour costs. As it was to be his personal residence, he took great care to ensure that everything was finished properly, with every baseboard well mitred and every trim-board properly applied. His professional pride demanded no less. When completed, it was one of the best-constructed houses on the street, and today, remains one of the most durable houses in the entire Kensington Market area.

We do not know why Thomas Crouch remained in residence for only two years. In 1889, Charles Lanning took possession of the house. In 1903, Mrs. Louise Rany and Thay Kent rented the house. I am confident that all the owners appreciated the home's quality construction.

The windows, veranda and door have all been replaced. The mansard roof has been covered with blue aluminum siding and the two gabled windows remain, facing the street. The brickwork of the large chimney, on the south side of the home, has been covered with cement or stucco. The moulding under the eaves has been removed. Today, the original character of the house is hidden, but it remains an attractive home nonetheless.

27 Bellevue Avenue.

Note:

The parking lot on the north side of 27 Bellevue can be entered through an opening in the stone wall, near the cement lamp post. At the far southeast corner of the parking lot, there is an opening in the fence, which allows access to a small alley. In the last century, it was named Augusta Place, and it extends eastward to Augusta Avenue

On Augusta Avenue, we leave behind the old Victorian Kensington, and examine the Jewish market, as well as the ethnic shopping district that has been superimposed over it.

The Jewish Market of Kensington

Though there were Jewish families living in Toronto before the turn of the twentieth century, they were relatively few in number. After 1900, this slowly changed as Jewish immigrants from Europe increased. Many were from Poland and Russia. Most arrived with little more than the clothes on their backs and meagre possessions in their suitcases. They had chosen a city that was predominately of British, Protestant origins and arrived in a decade when religious and ethnic tolerance was not a well-developed concept in society. As a result, they were mostly excluded from the mainstream institutions of society, and thus were marginalized.

Securing employment in the factories and shops of Toronto was not easy. To maintain a job in a gentile workplace, it was necessary to labour on Saturdays. Thus, the Jewish immigrants attempted to earn a living in a manner in which they were independent. If they took time off work to worship on the Sabbath, they would lose a day's income, but not their source of livelihood.

In the second decade of the twentieth century, Anglos were moving out of the homes in the Kensington area, seeking larger and newer residences further to the west, on streets such as Palmerston and Euclid. Kensington was close to the garment shops on Spadina, where many of the Jewish immigrants had found employment. The small homes of the area, built on narrow streets, were inexpensive to purchase. Extensions could easily be added to the rear of the houses. Single-family homes were often subdivided to provide space for several families, thus providing more assistance with the mortgage.

For many immigrants, the first method of starting a business was to sell goods from a knapsack on their back, walking the streets to reach the customers. As soon as they could, they acquired a pushcart, allowing them to carry larger amounts of merchandise. Many chose the "rag trade," as this was low in prestige and there was not much competition. Some gathered bottles, cleaned them, and resold them to factories. Others collected old sewing machines, repaired them, and resold them. They collected anything of value that was available and disposed of it for whatever price they could obtain.

Others sold fruit and vegetable from their carts. All these enterprises required almost no capital to commence and allowed the vendors to be free to worship on the Sabbath. When funds were available, stalls were built across the front of some of the small Kensington homes. Others opened stores in the front rooms of the houses. While the men pushed their carts through the streets, in weather that was often inclement, the women sold goods from these makeshift shops to earn extra income for the family.

Eventually modest extensions were constructed on the front of the homes, replacing the stalls and temporary shops. The Kensington Market was born. Merchants and their families lived above the stores or behind them. The district was slowly transformed from a quiet residential community into a vibrant shopping area with a European *shtetl* atmosphere. Despite its similarity to Jewish areas in other cities, such as the Lower East Side in New York or London's Whitechapel, Kensington was a unique creation, "one of a kind," and it remains this way today.

Today, many Victorian homes remain behind the commercial storefront. Gazing upward, one sees many of the peaked roofs and ornate trim of the old houses, although many have been severely altered. Augusta Avenue, Baldwin Street, St. Andrew's Avenue, and Kensington Avenue all contain examples of storefronts that extend from the houses to the edge of the sidewalks, where at one time the lawns were located.

Today, the Jewish market has mostly disappeared, and the small shops of yesteryear have become ethnic stores—West Indian, Latino, Caribbean, East Indian, and Portuguese. As well, Chinese and Korean merchants operate some of the stores.

The Amadeu's Restaurant, Portuguese Cuisine

182 and 184 Augusta (corner of Augusta and Denison Square)

The building where this restaurant is located was at one time a row of five small homes, which their Jewish owners converted into shops. The Amadeu's Restaurant occupies two of the old houses/shops. It was once the site of The Royal Fish Company, owned by Herbert and Abraham Katz. Nothing of the small houses remains in view today.

The Amadeu's Restaurant presents the decor, wines, and a menu of Lisbon, or one of the small villages of old Portugal, which faces the Atlantic Ocean, high above the rocky coastline. There are outdoor patios across the front of both buildings. The south patio accommodates the bar, and extends around to the south side. Beside it is the outdoor area for the restaurant.

186 and 188 Augusta Avenue

Until the summer of 2003, there was a faded sign above 188 Augusta that told of former days. Barely visible, it read, "Metro Meat and Delicatessen." Over fifty years ago, Leslie Adler operated a small meat market here. Throughout the years, many customers bought cold meats, sausages, and chickens in this store.

Today, the storefronts of 188 and 186 extend to the sidewalk. This is an example of the ethnic market of today having been superimposed on the Jewish market of yesteryear.

The House of Spices
190 Augusta

This was the fifth house in the row. In the early days of the Jewish market, the owners built a store across the front, and it extended from the house to the edge of the sidewalk. A modern-day store now occupies the same space.

The Original Hungry Thai Restaurant
196 Augusta Avenue

This is an excellent example of an old Victorian house that remains visible behind the modern addition, which they added to allow space for a commercial enterprise. In summer, this restaurant has a street patio. Peering inside, the steps reveal where the original front of the house was located. This is a Thai and Hungarian restaurant, and the menu has schnitzel, chicken paprika crepes, goulash soup, veggie pad Thai, as well as spring rolls.

202 Augusta Avenue

The modern white stucco storefront, with an apartment above, for many decades was the location of a bakery. It was an institution in the Kensington Market, and its owner a well-known member of the community.

Hyman Tepperman opened the bakery on this location in 1916. During the latter years of the First World War, he served residents of the market his fresh breads and pastries. He continued throughout the Second World War as well. In 1949, he renamed the shop New Style Bakery, and the following year he joined with Molly Pearl, and they operated the business together. In 1951, they changed the name to Molly Pearl's Bakery, but in 1956, they renamed it Continental Bakery, and they listed Hyman Tepperman as the proprietor. Orders for fresh bread could be reserved by telephoning the number EM 6-3604.

By this date, Mr. Tepperman had supplied bakery goods to the market for forty-three years. By 1966, the business was under the guidance of Mrs. S. Tepperman, and as she was employing her own initial in her name, it is assumed that Mr. Tepperman had passed away.

During the years when Kensington was predominantly Jewish, many children took great delight in entering this small bakery, hoping their parents would allow them to choose from the treats on display. Pennies were scarce, but few adults could refuse a child a sweet indulgence. For a child, choosing was a lengthy ritual that Mr. Tepperman and his wife likely endured with a mixture of impatience and amusement.

The bakery was a happy place and created cherished memories for those who entered the shop. Years later, many of the customers who frequented the bakery during the four decades of Mr. Tepperman's tenure, fondly remembered the tinkle of the bell above the door and the fragrance from the ovens

214 Augusta Avenue

The older house, behind the store, has interesting bargeboards (wooden trim) and a Gothic window in the peak. The red-brick house, set back from the street, at one time possessed a front lawn and likely a small garden. At the rear of the house, the first building addition is of brick, while the second addition is of wood. The side door (on the north side) has been bricked over. The rear extension (possible the original kitchen) has a rear door, side door, and two windows.

245 and 243 Augusta, East Side
Two semi-detached red-brick homes, set back from the street.

Jumbo Empanadas
245 Augusta

In 1930, this was the home of David Millar's family. In 1935, Philip Waxman, who owned College Men's Wear and the Peel Shirt Shop, occupied it. The home was eventually converted into a shop and today houses a small restaurant that serves Chilean food, specializing in empanadas. These are small baked pastries containing beef, chicken, or vegetables. The smaller empanadas have a cheese filling. An attractive patio is at the front of the establishment.

Freshmart
239–241 Augusta Avenue

In the early twentieth century, a synagogue sat on this location. In 1923, they demolished it, and constructed Zimmerman's Market, one of the earliest grocery stores in the area. Through the years, various shops were located here, including a large clothing store named "Fairland."

The Zimmerman family has now returned to the Kensington Market and has opened a supermarket. Many residents in the market protested against its opening, as they wished to safeguard the small-shop style of the area. Though such a large, modern-style store may appear out of place among the small shops of the market, for many, it provides necessities that the small stores do not stock.

235 Augusta Avenue
Northeast corner of Baldwin and Augusta (Casa Acoreana)

Louie's Kaffe is a small coffee shop on the west side of the building that houses Casa Acoreana. Although the owners are Portuguese, from the Azores, the small coffee shop seems reminiscent of the stalls found in the eastern Mediterranean lands, particularly in Greece or North Africa. Patrons sit on the stools placed out on the sidewalk and sip strong coffee while they discuss the events of the day. There is a curved bench on the

Augusta side of the cafe, where it is possible to sit and watch the world go by. No other spot in the market has the atmosphere of this small establishment. Though it is open to the elements, it is busy all winter long. On winter mornings, patrons huddle on the stools to engage in their favourite morning ritual—"coffee and conversation."

The building containing the coffee shop, on the northeast corner of Baldwin and Augusta, is one of the largest in the Kensington Market. It was originally the grocery store of L. Drilleck, whose business was taken over by Max Katz in 1924. Max remained here until 1929, then relocated to 195 Baldwin Street.

The building was empty until 1930, when Norman Young opened a store that sold dairy products. This same year, they altered the south façade of the building to create several small shops, which today still face Baldwin Street. These will be examined when we turn the corner.

Shop at the Northeast Corner of Augusta and Baldwin
235 Augusta Avenue

Building on the northeast corner of Augusta Avenue and Baldwin, which contains Louie's Kaffe and the shop with spices and nuts.

This shop proudly declares on its sign, "Nuts make the world go round." We assume that this is not a political statement. Luis Pavao commenced the business in 1955, and today it remains a family enterprise, now operated by his sons. The store exhibits an excellent display of nuts and has one of the city's finest assortments of rice. The odour of the spices fills the interior. Chocolate and dried fruits are also sold. The shelves extend to the ceiling, which is fourteen feet high. A long pole with a pincer on the end, capable of gripping objects, is required to retrieve bottles or jars from the top shelves.

The collection of spices is so complete that I overheard a visitor from the United States declare that he was able to purchase spices here that he had not been able to locate in either New York City or San Francisco. The assortment of candies, once referred to as "penny candy," is in large glass jars, and is one of the best assortments in all of Toronto.

This section of the Kensington Market has a concentration of shops that sell spices, nuts, and different varieties of rice. There are three more such stores further along the street.

View of Augusta Avenue looking south from near Baldwin Street in 1963. In this decade, vendors' stalls lined both sides of the street.

City of Toronto Archives, Series 1057, Item 5613

Baldwin Street

This street was named Agnes in the 1850s and renamed Clyde in the 1870s. They changed it to Baldwin in 1897, and made the postal addresses continuous with the section of Baldwin Street on the east side of Spadina. Baldwin Street derives its name from William Baldwin (1775–1844), the original owner of the mansion built on the hill overlooking Spadina Avenue.

206 Baldwin Street

This shop is located in the same building as Nuts. Though built in 1930, even as recently as 2009 it resembled a 1920s storefront, its thin wood frames supporting large glass windows. It was originally the poultry shop of A. Prussky, and in 1932, Sam Chalkin operated a similar business from this location.

Max and Son Meat Market occupied the site for many years. Established in 1955, it was one of the few stores remaining from the days when the market was predominantly Jewish. Many aspects of this shop reminded the customers of former days—the sawdust on the floor, two large wood butcher blocks, meat scales against the east wall, and large meat hooks hanging in the right-hand window. The white refrigerator formed a counter and displayed the meats. It was a store like our grandmothers visited and knew so well.

Max's son, Solly, operated the store for many years, having worked in it since he was sixteen. He retired in September 2009, one of the last Jewish shopkeepers remaining in the market. His departure marked the end of an era. One of the city's news stations sent a TV crew, and newspapers featured articles about the event.

The new owners of the business have respected the historic character of the property, and added vintage photographs to the shop interior. They offer a wide selection of quality meats and greet their customers in a manner reminiscent of the friendly style that Solly established.

The author wishes them success in their new endeavour.

Coral Sea Fish Market
198 Baldwin Street

This is a Caribbean-style fish market. The decorations on the building are colourful, especially the mural of a fisherman with a hook on the end of his arm, painted on the west wall in the laneway. The old man and the fish he is riding are smoking pipes. The other fish have cigarettes in their mouths. The mural promotes the merits of "smoked fish." It was on the wall in 2009, but we do not known how long it will remain before they replace it. Several different murals have been on this wall during the last five years.

Built of red bricks, the shop occupies one of a pair of houses. It was the home of Abraham Prussky, until Max Katz added a storefront and moved his grocery store here in 1929, after they had forced him to vacate the larger premises on the corner. He remained in this location until 1935, when he relocated once more, continuing his business in the store across the street at 195 Baldwin, which today is the "New Seaway Fish Market."

The mural on the west wall of the Coral Sea Fish Market at 198 Baldwin Street. The amusing graphics promote the merits of "smoked" fish.

Small Home at 200A Littlehayes Lane
Alley on the west side of Coral Sea Fish Market

The lane bears the name "Littlehayes," who in the 1790s was the owner of the park lot where today the Kensington Market is located. The history of this multi-home building is a mystery, as there is no reference to it in the old Toronto directories. The door of the dwelling faces the laneway. The top two floors resemble the architecture found in the Greek Islands, with their rectangular shape, small balconies, and flat rooftops.

On hot summer nights, the view from the top terrace of this laneway abode, overlooking the darkened market below, must surely be unique. The hustle and bustle of the daytime market is hushed and stilled. Except for the few twinkling lights below, there remain few signs of man's intrusion into the area.

However, in the distance is the rumble of the Spadina streetcars, and gazing beyond the market, the neon glitter of the downtown towers hovers on the horizon. It is a constant reminder that the Kensington Market is a confined area, harboured within a great metropolitan area—a village within.

Tom's Place
192 Baldwin Street

This clothing store occupies five old houses, numbers 192 to 186. In the market's Jewish era, storefronts were added to all five homes. Today, they have boarded up one of the storefronts in the row. Large skylights have been added to the roofs of the houses to allow more light in the showrooms on the second floor.

The store is operated by Tom Mikalik and is a regular supplier of clothes to the movie industry. In the credits shown at the conclusion of films produced in the Toronto area, it is common to see the name of the shop listed. It specializes in high-end labels, and its annual sales attract people from all over the city, who line up on the street at seven in the morning to secure the best bargains.

South Side of the Street

197 Baldwin Street

In the 1920s, this was the home of Mrs. Fannie Salamansky, a widow. In 1935, Mrs. Minnie Salem moved in with her. It is interesting to speculate on the thoughts of these two women, who were familiar with the area when it was the commercial centre of Toronto's Jewish population. When families relocated into residential area beyond the borders of the market, they witnessed the influx of shoppers from other parts of the city, as they came to purchase the kosher meats and other products familiar to them from the days before they immigrated to Canada.

In the 1920s, live ducks and chickens poked their necks between the slates of the wooden crates, while a proud rooster crowed its final "cock-a-doodle-do," its cry audible above the animated conversations of the shoppers. Merchants displayed an assortment of meats, pickles in large glass jars, breads, and fish, which lined the shop windows and the tables in the stalls in front of the storefronts on the streets. The sound of voices, carts, neighing horses, and clucking fowl pervaded the scene, creating a collage of noise and vibrant colours.

For the European immigrants who frequented the market in the 1920s and 1930s, the streets of Kensington created the familiarity of "home." Friends greeted one another, seeking news of the homeland, gleaned from a recently arrived letter. Young children born in Toronto had never seen the distant land of their parents, but they absorbed the stories and traditions, making them their own, never to be forgotten.

In 1938, Mrs. Minnie Salem sold the house and the new owners added a storefront. The home of the two women became the Royal Fish Market, and the owners expanded the business to incorporate 195 Baldwin Street. Today, number 197 is again a separate shop.

195 Baldwin Street

This structure may appear to be a new building, as modern brick has been laid over the old house. From the north side of the street, it is possible to view the peak of the former residence. In 1926, it became the Morris Caplin Fish Market, but the business failed and the premises were empty for two years. In 1928, Morris Caplin resumed his fish business. As previously mentioned, in 1935, Max Katz relocated his fish market here from across the street.

In the modern era, a Greek immigrant named Theodore owned the store. He earned is living in the market, and raised his family in the city. Today, he has retired and gone back to the sunny shores of his Mediterranean homeland. As of 2009, the new owners have retained the bold blue awning above the shop window. The store sells excellent Dover sole, fresh salmon, and fresh, plump mussels. I shop frequently at this store when I need to indulge my craving for fresh seafood.

Patty King
187 Baldwin

In 1920, this was the home of Samuel Gotlab, and in 1923, Philip Sroka opened a butcher shop at this location. Today it is a West Indian bakery, selling *ackee*, patties, and curried chicken. The warm beef patties, which come with either spicy or regular seasoning, are delicious on a cold winter morning when I shop in the market. Their spicy warmth dispels the dampness of the morn.

Because of modern additions to the building, no evidence of the original house remains in view today.

European Meat Market
176 Baldwin Street

In 1964, European Meats arrived in the Kensington Market, but only occupied the premises at 178 Baldwin Street. In 1985, the business expanded into the other shops (176 and 174). The famous meat market is now contained within two of the old row houses, and the original site (178) is used as the cutting and preparation room. Its windows are covered over.

The store's methods of operations have changed little from the old days of the Kensington Market. Transactions are conducted in metric and imperial. It requires three staff members to complete a transaction. First, customers take a number from a dispenser located on the right-hand side, near the door. They carry it to the counter and hand it to an employee, who lines them up and shouts the numbers in the order in which they are to be served. When a customer's number is called, it is then handed to another employee, who fills the order. When completed, the customer walks to the front of the store to the cashier, who accepts the money and places the meat in a plastic bag. The transaction is now complete.

This system is indeed a part of the Europe of earlier days, but is amazingly efficient. Sign language is often employed by the customers to denote the quantities desired, as on a busy day the store is so crowded that it is impossible to be heard above the clamour of voices.

The store has excellent strip loin steaks. The back bacon, hams, and cold cuts are truly excellent. People come from all over the city to purchase meat here. On a Saturday, it is jammed, and at Christmas time, the crowds are unbelievable.

I believe that shopping here is an experience to be savoured, not a chore to be endured.

172 Baldwin Street

In 1921, this was the home of Mr. S. Lebowitz, who earned his living selling dry goods. Perhaps he began in the business by operating a push cart and walking throughout the streets peddling clothes. In 1924, he had sufficient funds to open a bakery at 172 Baldwin Street. In 1935, the bakery was purchased by Samuel Lottman, who operated it under the name Imperial Bakery. Eventually he relocated to larger premises across the street.

For many years this was the site of My Market Bakery. It sold delicious bagels, pastries, and bread. It eventually relocated to 184 Baldwin Street, where today I frequently purchase sun-dried tomato bread, black olive sourdough bread, and fresh baguettes.

170 Baldwin

In 1920, this was the home of Louis Selenick, and in 1924, it became the residence of Benjamin Shapiro. He moved away in 1926, and the house was unoccupied until the following year, when Nathan and Annie Greenberg bought the premises. Annie was widowed in 1935, and during the following year the house was again empty. In 1937, Steve Lukachev's family lived here, and then, in 1938, they shared the dwelling with Isaac Itzkowitz's family.

In 1940, Joseph Sidney and Mrs. Mary Lukachev converted the premises into a fruit store, and the extension they built on the home remains visible today. It is now a bar, specializing in country and western music, and in the evenings features a live band. Inside there is a large poster of Elvis Presley and an upright piano. The small tables for the patrons were covered with tablecloths with a leopard-skin pattern. Despite the bar's emphasis on country and western music, the atmosphere is reminiscent of Bourbon Street in New Orleans. Outside there is a narrow patio for customers to enjoy a drink while observing the view on the street.

Kensington Market attracts diverse personalities. On a summer day in the market, I overheard a young man explaining to a friend the correct way to drink rum. He stated that the bottle should be placed in a paper bag, and one pant leg should be rolled up to the knee. A headband should be worn, and one's shirt should be unbuttoned to the navel.

It is small wonder that the market contains so many colourful characters. Carrying alcoholic drinks on the street, though illegal in Ontario, is a true part of the French Quarter in New Orleans. However, some of the customers of 170 Baldwin Street similarly appreciate the relaxed environment of Kensington.

Kensington Community Centre
160 Baldwin Street

Among the clothing shops located on the ground floor within the condominium at 160 Baldwin is the Kensington Community Centre, where they make the lanterns for the annual Festival of the Lights. The parade travels throughout the streets of the market after sunset on the winter solstice. It is an impressive and haunting sight to see hundreds of people, many with young children, marching throughout the streets, their small lights shining brightly in the blackness of the night. Each December 21st, I try to join the throngs of people who line the sidewalks to enjoy this ancient recognition of the beginning of winter.

Other workshops offered at the community centre are shadow puppetry, tie-dye making, and sessions for children including singing and acting lessons.

171 Baldwin, South Side

This store is contained within an addition to the old house, which in 1923 David Kwosnewski owned. A person can view the roof of the home from the opposite side of the street. Various families owned the house until 1958, when they opened Baldwin Kosher Meat Market on the premises. It remained in business for over a decade.

The present occupant is Caribbean Corner, an excellent place to purchase sorrel, a Caribbean berry that the islanders use to make a Christmas drink. The fresh berries arrive in December, but the dried (preserved) berries are available year-round. They make the drink by pouring hot water on the berries, adding cinnamon, and then sugaring it to taste. Jamaicans usually add ginger to the beverage.

The store also sells plantain and sugar cane and arranges money transfers, mainly to the Caribbean. On Saturday mornings, especially near Christmas, it is crowded with customers, anxious to purchase its unique and varied products.

173 Baldwin Street

In 1923, this was the home of Abraham Urman, and, in 1935, it became the residence of Nathan Shekter. It remained in residential use until 1958 but became vacant in 1959. In 1960, it was the site of the Import Food Company. In 1962 it was Palla's Tropical Foods, operated by Spiros Kanelopoulos. He continued in business at this location until 1976, when Peter Goudas took it over.

Peter Goudas had many West Indian customers, who informed him of which products they wished to have imported from the islands. The store became so successful that Peter relocated to larger premises outside the market area. The "Goudas" label was born.

For many years, the Baldwin Grocery Store occupied 173 Baldwin Street.

175 Baldwin Street, South Side

There is a crest on the facade of the building, which is the same one as on 168 Baldwin Street. In addition, the detailing pattern under the wood trim at the top is the same on both buildings. Likely, they were constructed by the same builder.

From 1917 until 1937, this was the bakery of Aaron Perlmutter. A close examination of the green awning (as of 2009) reveals that it was at one time The Caribbean Sea Fish Market.

179 Baldwin Street

This modern, white building was at one time the site of Lottman's Imperial Bakery (now demolished). It had been previously been located across the street.

Note:

On Baldwin Street, looking east toward Spadina, one is able to view the old houses on the east side of Spadina, with shops on the ground-floor level. These homes are a storey and a half and have white gingerbread trim on the peaks. In the 1870s, the style was popular in Ontario for farm homes.

Kensington Avenue

In the 1850s, Kensington Avenue was named Elizabeth Street. In the 1880s, they called it Vanauley Street. It commenced at Queen Street and ended at Baldwin Street. In this decade, a section of Vanauley, between Grange Avenue and Dundas Street, was open fields. Because the fields divided the street into two sections, the part north of Dundas became known as Upper Vanauley. In 1890, it was changed to Kensington Avenue. Today Vanauley still commences at Queen Street, but it only extends one block north.

By the 1920s, Kensington Avenue had become the heart of the Jewish market. Today fruit and vegetable stores and two cheese shops exist alongside some of the hippest shops in Kensington. Signs advertise retro and vintage clothing.

**Fruit and vegetable market on the northeast corner of
Kensington Avenue and St. Andrews Street, looking
north on Kensington Avenue toward Baldwin Street.**

Mendel's Creamery and Global Cheese Shop
72 and 76 Kensington, respectively

These two cheese shops are located in a new building, the former houses on the site having been demolished by fire. A wide variety of cheeses is sold by both shops, which carry more than three hundred varieties. Prices are reasonable.

To a customer who is unfamiliar with a variety of cheese, the sellers give a free sample. In the left-hand window of Global Cheeses is a collection of colourful Portuguese and Italian ceramic dishes, including plates and bowls. The shop presents a colourful and interesting display to those who pass on the street.

I personally believe that the world would be a better place if it contained more shops like Mendel's Creamery. The friendly service and kind regard that the staff offers to their customers are not to be found in the large supermarkets and bulk stores of today. I truly hope this cheese shop never disappears from the market scene.

As you might have guessed, I frequently visit this establishment.

Sanci's
68 Kensington

In the early years of the twentieth century, this was the location of the butcher shop of Louis Sakovitch, who remained in business here until 1923. In 1924, Morris Deutch opened a fish market. In 1926, it became the poultry shop of Max Bronstein, and the following year it was the dry goods store of G. H. Galperin.

His business folded in 1928, and the premises remained vacant in 1929, the year the Great Depression began. In 1930, Louis Herman opened a poultry business, but times were difficult and he was not successful. In 1931 Salvatore and Antonina Sanci bought the store.

Since 1914, before moving to Kensington Avenue, Salvatori (Samuel) Sanci had operated a fruit market at Queen and Bay, which he later relocated to Yonge near Carlton Street. He was reputed to have been the first merchant in Toronto to import bananas. As mentioned, in 1931, he opened his shop on Kensington Avenue, specializing in fruits from the Caribbean.

Salvatori, who preferred to be called Samuel, was the first Italian merchant in the area. In 1937, he extended the store front and discreetly placed the design of a cross in the brickwork at the top of the building. It is this shop that exists today. The 1914 date on the front of the store refers to the date that Salvatore started his business in Toronto, not the year he arrived at this location.

68 Kensington Avenue.

Kensington Meats
63 Kensington Avenue

A shoe store occupied this quaint shop in the early 1920s. In 1925, it was taken over by Hyman Silverbirk, who operated it as a grocery store. In 1927, Ana Feldman bought the business and sold groceries from the site until 1934. Max Swartz, another grocer, became the owner in 1935, but by the following year he had vacated the premises. The store was empty in 1936. In 1937, Benjamin Applebaum reopened it as a fruit and vegetable store.

It is now a meat market, but it retains the atmosphere and appearance of a shop of yesteryear. Personally, I have found the owner of the shop to be helpful and pleasingly chatty. The lamb steaks that I have purchased here have been tender and flavourful. It is one of the market's little-known jewels.

Note:

Kensington Place, formerly Mackenzie Place, is a small laneway that leads west from Kensington Avenue. It is opposite St. Andrew Street, between 44 and 46 Kensington Avenue. It is a public walkway.

Kensington Place is another example of the concept of a "home behind a home." It was a way of providing accommodation to families at a less expensive price than if the dwellings had been constructed on a street. There are no homes listed in the Toronto directories for this location prior to 1890. Either the homes were not constructed before that year, or they were not listed.

22 Kensington Place

In 1890, this home was occupied by John J. Varney, a barber by trade. It is perhaps the most interesting house in the row. In the modern era, it was purchased by a family from the Azores, who placed roughcast (cement and sand) over the façade, painted it yellow, and added fish and ducks to the design. He allowed his children to place their names (Nico and Fev) in the cement to the left of the door. The names are still visible, as well as their handprints and footprints. The work is signed MCE, and above the lower window are the numbers 6-38. These are likely his birth date. The work is dated 8-95.

The tiles displaying the postal number are blue and white, and there is a bright blue door, perhaps reminding the owner of his island home. The upper door has creative netting across it, an art form in the Azores. There is a wooden cover over the mail slot.

22 Kensington Place.

28 Kensington Place

In 1890, William H. Grabhill lived at this address. He was employed by firm of Ewart and Johnson, a company that manufactured carriages and wagons. It is worth noting the fancy gingerbread trim on the eaves and the small veranda, which is quite impressive for such a small home.

30 Kensington Place

David Sigley, a streetcar conductor, resided in this house in 1890. Although today this home is covered with aluminum siding, the configuration of the windows and door remain true to the original design. In most of the other houses, they have been altered. The windows are quite large, as the dwelling was built in an era without electricity. The transom window over the door allowed light into the narrow hallway. The spool and spindle woodwork on the veranda reflects the designs of earlier decades.

The residents have placed a charming ornament, a red cat, on the veranda roof of the home.

Note:

Returning to Kensington Avenue, at the southern end of the street there are many interesting shops.

44 Kensington Avenue

West side, south side of the laneway entrance

The 1868–1869 Toronto directories reveal that the building lot where 42 Kensington is located was an empty field. In 1870, the house was constructed, and was occupied by Miss Ann Johnson, a dressmaker. Its original postal address was 130 Vanauley. In 1890, the name of the street and the postal number was changed to 44 Kensington Avenue.

It is a bay-and-gable design, although the bay window on the first floor has been replaced. The second-floor windows have been altered. The wooden trim in the peak is the only feature of the original home that is evident, as the façade is covered with brick siding.

42 Kensington Avenue

During the 1850s, north of Dundas Street, there were no houses on the street. In 1861, 42 Kensington Avenue was constructed, although in that year its address was 130 Vanauley Street. George Gibson, who earned his living as a trader, purchased the house, but he remained in residence at 97 St. Patrick Street (Dundas Street West). The following year, he moved into the house, along with Mrs. Mary O'Brien, a widow. It is likely that they were related.

The extension on the front was possibly built in the 1920s or 1930s. The old chimney remains on the south side of the steep roof. The brickwork at the top of the 1930's façade is painted in a dramatic blue and red.

30 and 32 Kensington Avenue

These charming late-Victorian homes, with their ornate verandas, were built between the years 1873 and 1874. The first resident of number 30 was Thomas Churchill, and number 32 was Alexander Clark, an engineer. The porch-supports (pillars) of the houses are decorative, as are the gingerbread trim and spool work. The storm doors complement the style, although it is likely that they are modern replacements. They are bay-and-gable homes, although the first-floor window of number 32 has been altered. On the third floor of number 32 there is a small balcony.

When they built these homes, Canada's economy was in a slump. Families rarely travelled far from home in the best of times, and during difficult days they remained particularly close to their neighbourhoods. Their travels were limited to simply strolling along the quiet streets of the community.

In an era without automobiles and electric lighting, when darkness folded around the verandas of 30 and 32 Kensington Avenue, on warm evenings the children sat on the veranda steps. As their parents engaged in "adult talk," the youngsters teased each other and told humorous stories about the day's activities. Sometimes they called to a friend across the street, and their parents told them to be less boisterous. A passing adult elicited attention from the children, as they too longed for the freedom to amble along the avenue after sunset, free of supervision.

Kensington Avenue was within a quiet, comfortable neighbourhood, despite sitting on the edge of the busy market scene. Families lived in close proximity, assisting each other in troubling times. They knew each other's foibles and misadventures, and though gossip was also a part of "veranda life," it was usually mischievous rather than cruel. The community existed and lived their days in relative harmony.

In some respects, this remains true of the market area today.

Numbers 30 and 32 Kensington Avenue.

Note:

A street sign shows the laneway Fitzroy Terrace, going west off St. Kensington Avenue. Fitzroy Terrace first appeared in the city directories in 1890. At the end of the laneway, is another example of "a house behind a house."

5, 6, 7, and 8 Fitzroy Terrace

These homes are further examples of small dwellings that were constructed to house immigrant workers who came to Canada from the British Isles.

The postal numbers are unusual in that they are consecutive, rather than either odd or even, as is the usual custom. The houses are similar in design to those in Kensington Place.

The house with the postal address number 5 was built in 1890, and the numbers 6, 7, and 8 were constructed the following year.

3 Fitzroy Terrace

This home first appeared in the Toronto directories in 1890. Its architectural style was popular for farmhouses in rural Ontario throughout the 1850s and 1860s. Because of the style, it is possible that they constructed this house prior to 1890, but the Toronto directories do not list it.

Duncan Morrison, a labourer occupied it in 1890. Vernacular Doric pilasters are on either side of the door.

3 Fitzroy Terrace.

1 Fitzroy Terrace

In 1890, this house was under construction. The following year, Samuel Oakley, a stonecutter by trade, moved into the premises. During the earlier months of the year, he had lived at 20 Kensington Avenue, where he had shared the house. He likely welcomed the move to the laneway behind the other houses, as he now occupied a home on his own.

Today, only the rooftop of the house is visible, as a high fence blocks the home from view. A person can see the postal number on the gate.

Leaving Fitzroy Terrace and Returning to Kensington Avenue

20 and 22 Kensington Avenue

These two semi-detached homes, built from 1889 to 1890, were set back from the street and at one time had lawns in front of them. They have now joined the two buildings into a single store, and the brickwork painted it a bright yellow (as of 2009). In the peak there are attractive bargeboards (trim). On the north side, the windows have been removed, but they remain in the extension at the rear.

In 1890, 20 Kensington Avenue was occupied by Robert Butler, the assistant manager at Standard Manufacturing Company, and Samuel Oakley, a stonecutter by trade. By the end of the year, Oakley had relocated to Fitzroy Terrace, where, as mentioned, he occupied the entire house.

14 Kensington Avenue

This colourful store is painted blue, and possesses a sunburst pattern high in the peak of the gable. The original home was constructed 1873, and the storefront was added during the last century.

In 1873, the house's occupant was Samuel Vance, a partner in the firm of Oag and Vance, Engineers and Machinists. A professional man, he was able to purchase a home in this new and up-and-coming neighbourhood. It was a great area to raise a family, away from the squalid downtown streets, where open fields for children to play were rare.

2 Kensington Avenue

This home was built 1888, but remained unsold. In 1889, it was purchased by James Stewart, an engineer with the Grand Trunk Railway. It was the golden age of steam locomotives, as they extended branch railway lines into small towns. The government maintained roads poorly, as the era of the automobile had not yet dawned. The railway lines were the only practical means of travel between distant points, where horse and cart were impractical.

To the children of Kensington Avenue, Mr. Stewart was part of an exciting occupation. When he returned home from work, they observed him as he wearily trod up the street. They thought about his exciting day in the cab of his giant engine, as it roared along the tracks, pouring smoke and steam over the countryside. The hollow echo of the train's whistle, sometimes heard on a quiet evening, was a sound that caused their imaginations to soar. Every child dreamed of participating in this wondrous mode of travel.

Mr. Stewart's house has a high-peaked gable. It is another bay-and-gable house, with a cornucopia-like design in the peak and fancy wooden trim on the sides of the third-floor windows. The frames around the door and transom window appear to be the original, but the glass has been replaced in both windows.

15 Kensington Avenue, Residential, East Side

The house was built in 1874, and Joshua Payne was its first resident. In an age of ever-expanding residential construction, he earned his living as a moulder. His services were in constant demand. In this era, a builder contracted to construct one or two houses, and the combined skills of his men performed all the tasks necessary to complete the house. They had not yet conceived the idea of mass-produced, cookie-cutter housing developments. They designed and built each home individually, exhibiting great pride in their workmanship.

This home at 15 Kensington Avenue is a fine example of a house of the era. The original veranda, and door survive, painted in dark tones of green and red. There is interesting modern tile work on the veranda steps. The bricks have been covered with yellow paint, and high in the peak there is a hand-cut floral pattern.

19 Kensington Avenue

This house has a sign on it that states it is a 1890s home. However, the Toronto directories reveal that in 1871–1872, a house on this site was occupied by William Johnson, a painter. It's possible that this was an earlier dwelling.

The veranda is one of the finest preserved in the entire area. The pink and green trim, as well as the dentils under the veranda's eaves, create a very pleasant effect. The brickwork has been cleaned, restoring the dwelling to its original appearance. Cut designs are in the wood trim at the apex of the peak, and at both sides at the bottom of the peak. Often there is a black and white cat curled up sleeping in the window. The shop specializes in jewellery.

St. Andrew Street

St. Andrew Street was named after the patron saint of Scotland. It was one of the first streets cut through the fields west of Spadina Avenue. It appears on the city maps of 1858 but is shown as St. Andrews. The Toronto directory of 1875 lists it as St. Andrew's. Today, the sign at the west end of the street name spells the name as "St. Andrew," but on the east end (at Spadina), the sign shows "St. Andrews." Perhaps this inconsistency reflects the eccentricity that has become a trademark of the Kensington Market.

Shampoo
32 St. Andrew Street

The beauty salon and gift shop are within a building extension attached to the front of a Victorian house, built in 1888, its first occupant being Hiland Hancock. The home's gabled peak soars high above the shop. There is a small dormer window protruding from the roof. At the ground level, if you peek inside, you will see the bay window of the original house. The merchant advertises that the gifts sold within are "impossibly hip."

Moon Bean Coffee Company
30 St. Andrew Street

This coffee house is one of the most interesting in the city, contained within a house that was built in 1873. It was unoccupied in 1874, but the following year, Thomas Peters, a labourer, moved into the premises.

The Moon Bean cafe roasts and grinds its own beans. The smoke from a small metal chimney above the roaster allows the smell of the coffee to permeate the air for a considerable distance, carrying on the breeze to the surrounding shops. I cannot express the degree of pleasure that I have experienced on cool mornings when I turn the corner at Spadina and walk along St. Andrew's Street, savouring the rich bouquet of the fresh coffee.

The tops of the small tables inside consist of solid pine planks that have been cut to size. Make sure to visit the back room, as it is an opportunity to experience the inside of a rear building extension typical of the houses in that era. In the outside rear patio, you can view similar extensions on the other houses. They usually contained the kitchens of the homes. In the front patio of the "Moon Bean," you may enjoy a cup of coffee and watch the shoppers and residents pass by on the street.

In the roof, there is a gable to allow light into the third-floor level. One of the modillions (brackets) under the eave is missing. However, this is the only thing the cafe lacks. Modern coffee chain stores cannot hold a candle to this inimitable establishment.

30 St. Andrew Street.

St. Andrew's Poultry
17 St. Andrew Street

Across the street from the Moon Bean Coffee Company, on the south side of the street, is a modern building. The site has a history that goes far back into the past.

In 1856, there were only three houses on St. Andrew's Street, and the site of number 17 was a vacant lot. By 1864, there were four houses on the south side of St. Andrew's Street, the additional home being the one on the site of number 17. In the mid-1860s, a blacksmith shop occupied the property.

Today, a modern building has been built on the location. St. Andrew's Poultry is an excellent place to purchase fresh chicken and turkey. As of 2009, the tongue-in-cheek mural on the outside west wall of the building was worth examining. Entitled the "Cirque de Poulet," ringmaster Coc Au Vin shares the stage with various performers: "Mince Carter, Chesty LaRue, White Feather the Mystique, Chucky Flameback, and George's Bouillon." These colourful names match the colourful individuals who stroll around the market of today, especially "Chesty LaRue."

The roasting chickens I have purchased at this store have been the best I have ever found. Whenever I travel to other cities and countries, I employ St. Andrew's Poultry as my standard of comparison.

The tongue-in-cheek mural on the wall of St. Andrew's Poultry, at 17 St. Andrew's Street, a project of Cecil/Harbourfront GTA

Note:

Observe the laneway between the large yellow Chinese restaurant and #13 St. Andrew Street.

Peering down this small lane there is a view of the back of the small houses on Glen Baille Place, another example in the Kensington Market area of the concept of "a house behind a house." This narrow street exits on Spadina Avenue.

The Minsker Synagogue

Immigrants from Russia, especially the Minsk area, formed the original congregation in 1912 to follow the Orthodox practices of their Jewish faith. Records reveal that in 1913 it had fifty members, but as more immigrants settled in the Kensington area, the congregation grew.

They purchased two houses on St. Andrews Street, which they joined to create a single space, and gathered there to worship. During the 1920s, they raised funds to erect a new building. Eventually, the congregation was able to demolish the two old houses, and they completed the new synagogue in 1930.

Inspired by a synagogue in Poland, the architect created a symmetrical design, with impressive central doors. The façade has three sections, with parapets above them. Inside the synagogue, there is a balcony where women and children sit when attending services. It is the only Orthodox synagogue remaining in the downtown area that has a full-time rabbi offering morning prayers every day of the week.

**The Minsker Synagogue on St. Andrews
Street in the Kensington Market.**

Bright Pearl Seafood Restaurant
Southwest Corner of St. Andrew and Spadina

This Chinese restaurant employs paint and small tiles in colours of yellow and red to create an oriental appearance. To add to this effect, it has green tiles on the roof. Two fierce white lions guard either side of the steps.

Originally, there were two houses on this site. In the 1920s, they were converted to create the Toronto Labour Lyceum, a meeting hall for the Jewish workers in the garment industry. In 1929, more space was needed, so a new front and larger meeting rooms were added. The building was a focal point of the community, as it represented dressmakers as well as fur, cloak, and hat makers. It also served as a dance hall for the members.

An important event occurred in the hall on May 15, 1940. A funeral was held for Mrs. Emma Goldman, a well-known feminist, "anarchist," and critic. She had been a tireless lecturer who promoted planned parenthood and the legalization of birth control—very controversial issues during those days. The press often commented on her lectures, especially when she attacked the policies of Stalin and the Soviet Union. Having previously lived in the United States, she moved to Toronto when her American citizenship was revoked. She lived for a few years at 665 Spadina Avenue, and later relocated to 295 Vaughan Road, where she died of a stroke on May 14, 1940. The following day, a memorial service was held for her in the Labour Lyceum Hall, where the crowds were so great that they lined the sidewalks along Spadina Avenue.

In the 1950s, the Lyceum Building was extended, and another hall was added on the second floor. In the early 1970s, the union relocated to Cecil Street, and the site became the first Jewish old people's home.

In the years ahead, they sold the building and eventually the buyers re-opened it as a restaurant. Its colourful exterior reveals no hint of its past, when it was an important centre in the lives of the Jewish community.

*

The narrow streets of the Kensington Market reflect over a century of the history of Toronto. In addition, it is a visual record of the city's transition from a bastion of Anglo-Saxon Protestant culture to the multi-ethnic urban centre of today. The ethnic and retro markets of today have been superimposed over the old Jewish market of the past.

I hope the Kensington never loses its unique buildings, with their stores that create the atmosphere of bygone days. It is one of the best places in the city to shop for unusual clothing, purchase imported foods, enjoy a cup of coffee, partake of an ethnic meal, or just stroll to enjoy the flavour of the area. In summer, on "pedestrian Sundays," cars are banned from the streets, and a carnival atmosphere develops.

When I shop within its precincts, I am reminded of the neighbourhood of my youth, when Toronto was a considerably smaller and more personal city. In Kensington, people converse, laugh, complain, berate, and encourage. It is an environment where I feel at home.

Of all Toronto's "inner villages," for me, it is perhaps the most unique.

Chapter Five:

Queen Street West

Queen Street West District is located on Queen Street West between University Avenue and Bathurst Street. The section included in this study is from Spadina on the west, to University Avenue on the east.

Thoughts about Queen Street West

Christopher Hutsul wrote in the Toronto Star on August 29, 2004:

> Queen St., in effect is becoming one vast accidental urban success story. In richness and scale, there may be no better street in the world than our very own Queen Street.
>
> "I can't think of another street that has vitality, the variety, and has the length and the depth that Queen has from one end to the other," says Dr. Mitchell Kosny of Ryerson's School of Regional and Urban Planning. "It's starting to fill in."
>
> It might seem bold to pit Queen Street against the world's top strips but, in its way, it stacks up against the best of the best. Broadway in New York City starts out hot, then cools as it wends its way to Albany. Champs-Elysees in Paris is one of the world's most famous streets, but it's also a major thoroughfare. Highbrow visitors can enjoy the expensive restaurants and boutiques, but the average Parisian would head somewhere more accessible.
>
> Admittedly, our humble Queen Street might have a tough time out-classing La Ramblas in Barcelona, which, with its stunning architecture and endless culinary offerings, is one of the greatest streets in the world.

However, could it match Queen's understated, New World charm?

Certainly Queen Street reigns over Yonge Street, which is often considered our flagship route. "I don't see Yonge St. as having all that much continuity at all," says Kosny. "It doesn't have anywhere the life and vitality that Queen St. has." And while downtown has been busy evolving into a mini Times Square (as if that were something worth emulating), Queen St. has quietly grown out of its awkward years.

More thoughts about Queen Street West:

"One must look west from University Avenue on Queen Street to capture the visual flavour of old downtown."

—M. Kluchner,
Toronto the Way It Was
(Toronto: Whitecap Books, 1988)

"'Arrogantly Shabby' is the motto of Pawley's Island, South Carolina. The same might apply to Toronto's Queen Street West."

— Robert Frazier, Atlanta, Georgia

"London England's Carnaby Street is Britain's Queen Street West. Pity they lack the real thing!"

—The author

Queen Street is perhaps the liveliest and most interesting street in the city, a destination for Torontonians and tourists alike, a Mecca of trendy restaurants, sidewalk cafes, bizarre shops, and exotic boutiques. Young people have voted the Black Bull's patio the most popular outdoor drinking venue in the city.

Many visit Queen Street West simply to observe the eclectic mixture of people strolling along the crowded sidewalks, a few displaying unusual attire. Some believe that the outfits worn by the older tourists are even more outlandish.

The street is a place to connect with others. Sometimes a new friend is found or an old acquaintanceship renewed. Each spring the sweet scent of marijuana drifts lazily in the warm air. Bare flesh and body jewellery bloom in profusion, displayed on parts of the body that were well hidden during the winter months.

Adding to the street's hip and cool image, one of the city's most expensive eateries offers its clientele valet service to park their cars. By contrast, street people, who wear special outfits of their own, retrieve cigarette butts and beg spare coins as they hover in doorways or position themselves in favourite locations beside the curb or under a tree. They watch the affluent and young pass by sporting their trendy outfits, many of them clutching a container of specialty coffee or the odd hand-rolled joint. Few streets in the city exhibit such contrast.

When the brightness of the day fades to the soft light of evening, garish neon signs become more prominent. Well-worn doorways lead to stairs that ascend to the second-floor levels. The thumping beat from gigantic speakers intrudes into the night air like rhythmic tribal drums of a long-lost civilization. The sights and sounds lure the youthful crowd, enticing them to seek entrance to the pubs, bars, and restaurants. For some, the evening's goal is to attend the ever-popular Rivoli, and listen to the music of a not-yet-famous group, or to experience a popular underground comedian. Not until the early hours of the morning will the party crowd depart the scene, and even then, they will likely seek an after-hours club or quasi-illegal booze can. There is the endless cycle of nightlife on Queen Street West that is unrivalled throughout the city.

However, during the daylight hours, the street displays another scene, one that few are aware of it, as they rarely raise their eyes above the ground-floor level of the buildings. The upper storeys are rich in architectural detail and history. Gables, pointed dormers, parapets, tall brick chimneys, and ornate cornices with dentils and modillions gaze down silently on a streetscape that is foreign to the time that created them.

The hip Queen Street scene of today resembles a movie set superimposed on an ancient background. However, the original nineteenth-century stage remains amazingly intact, although a visitor must ignore the numerous modern-day actors and props if they wish to discover the former days of this fascinating street. This is one of the few Victorian commercial streetscapes that remains in Toronto. The city has designated it a Heritage Preservation Area. To explore its architecture is to enter a doorway into the past.

The Establishment of the Town of York

The town of York that Governor Simcoe planned in 1793 consisted of ten square blocks at the eastern end of today's Toronto harbour. Some of the names of the original streets changed throughout the years ahead; therefore, to avoid confusion in this study, I have mostly employed the modern names (Lot Street is the main exception).

Shortly after Simcoe had established York, he granted one-hundred-acre park lots beyond the town limits to influential and wealthy friends such as John Beverley Robinson, J. Russell, the Honourable A. Grant, R. J. D. Grey, J. Powell, and the Honourable Peter Russell. It was an attempt to emulate the great rural estates of Britain. The reality of residing in the wilderness of Upper Canada failed to thwart the grandiose dreams of the founder of York.

In 1797, because the settlers already occupied most of the town's building sites, and since the settlement was continuing to expand, it was evident that a new town plan was necessary. They decided to expand beyond the western boundary of the old town (George Street) and incorporate the forested lands to the west, as far as today's Peter Street.

They realized that a new roadway would be needed to the north of Richmond Street to cut through the newly incorporated territory. It would allow the town to expand and establish access to the free land grants. Simcoe ordered the military engineers to establish a surveyor's line westward, north of the town. They named the roadway along the surveyor's line Lot Street, because it formed the southern boundary of the park lots. The lots extended as far north as the Bloor Street of today. Lot Street was eventually renamed Queen Street.

For several years, the section of Lot Street east of today's Church Street remained incomplete because of Taddle Creek, which contained swamps and bogs with swarms of mosquitoes, the source of malaria. After they built Lot Street, York commenced extending westward. Homes and shops appeared along the new thoroughfare, and the street provided easy access to the old town and facilities such as the St. Lawrence Market, St. James Cathedral, and the shops of King Street. The area of Lot Street west of Yonge became known as the New Town, and rivalry developed between the old and new. Gradually, they built more shops and homes along Lot Street and it soon became a main thoroughfare.

Lot Street

In the early days, to refer to Lot Street as a "street" required a degree of wishful thinking on the part of the residents of York. In spring it was a perpetual sea of mud, and in the summer it was dusty, as well as full of holes and rocks. The rough and uneven surface was made worse by the ponderous wagons, whose wheels formed deep ruts as they tumbled over rocks or around boulders and stumps. In 1800, the city passed the Stump Act, which required those arrested for drunken behaviour to remove a stump from the roadway, but unfortunately, the law did not inspire temperance, and despite this harsh measure, during the years ahead the streets did not improve to any measurable degree.

Throughout the following two decades, the condition of the streets of the town, including Lot Street, changed very little. However, to widen the road, they gradually removed more trees. In 1835, the city council passed a law that street corners were to have four-foot-wide paving stones. However, judging by the amount of money spent, very few intersections were completed.

In Edwin C. Guillet's *Toronto, Trading Post to Great City* (Ontario Publishing Company, Toronto, 1934), a resident of York during the early years described the streets as "wretchedly paved, or not all, and were generally in a very bad condition. All the sidewalks were of wood, and in the principal streets were from eight to ten feet in width, the planks being laid crosswise, and on many of the private streets not more than four planks (four feet) in width, laid lengthwise. The nails frequently became loose, causing the ends to tilt, making it somewhat risky for pedestrians. These sidewalks had to be frequently renewed."

Another resident wrote, "Few who now stroll down the well-boarded sidewalks ... reflect upon the inconvenience attending this recreation to their sires and grandsires and granddames, who were compelled to tuck up their garments and pick their way from tuft to stone to stone. It was no unusual sight to behold a heavy lumber wagon sticking fast in the mud up to the axle in the middle of the street ... The party going portion of the citizens were content either to trudge it, or be shaken in a cart drawn by two sturdy oxen." Such was Lot Street during the early years of the town.

In 1834, the elected councillors changed the name York to Toronto. However, this did little to improve the condition of its streets and roadways. With the incorporation of the young city, for purposes of electing members to the city council and for voting, they designated four areas as wards. Lot Street became the dividing line between two of them—St. Andrew's and St. Patrick's. St. Andrew's commenced on the south side of Queen Street and extended south to King Street. St. Patrick's was on the north side and included the land as far north as Bloor Street. These boundaries remain essentially the same today.

Lot Street Is Renamed Queen Street

In 1837, following the death of her uncle, King William IV, Queen Victoria ascended the British throne, commencing the Victorian period of British history. The Empire greatly rejoiced and celebrated her coronation. In Toronto a whole ox was roasted in Market Square, at King and Jarvis Streets, the crowds remaining until the early hours of the morning. In 1843, it was decided to rename Lot Street to honour the young monarch, and Queen Street was born.

In the year the street was renamed, it was the northern boundary of Toronto. Because of the increase in land values, by this year some of the owners of the park lots subdivided their land and sold the property that fronted on Queen Street. The small parcels of land allowed modest buildings to be constructed.

Most of the structures were two storeys in height, with business enterprises on the ground floor and the owners living above their shops. North of Queen Street was mainly open fields and forested lands belonging to the various park lots. To the west, between Spadina and Bathurst, there were very few homes or businesses. The dwelling of James Fitzpatrick was an exception.

*

In 1840, homes on Queen Street remained few and scattered, with many vacant lots in between. According to an ordinance approved by the town council ten years earlier, the city hired Mr. George Walton to place numbers on the façades of the houses and buildings, Mr. Walton wrote the numbers on the buildings with a piece of chalk, and soon the markings disappeared. As the years progressed, and houses changed hands, many problems became evident.

The following was written by George Brown in reference to Queen Street, and was contained in the Toronto directory of 1846–1847:

> By the plan of the Corporation, where vacant lots occur, a given space is allowed for a [house] number, to prevent any disturbance of the order arising from the erection of new houses on such lots. In some instances, this plan has not been strictly adhered to; indeed, it was almost impossible for a person without accurately measuring the ground, to place the numbers properly.

When buildings were erected on vacant land, some were larger than anticipated, while others were smaller, as more than one home had been constructed on a single lot. As a result, the numbers did not always progress sequentially. Through the decades, as property prices increased on Queen Street, merchants sometimes purchased half lots, and then extended the shops as far back as possible. This created many long, narrow buildings, many of which still stand today. Half-numbers (e.g., 303½) were sometimes employed, and at other times, the lack of proper sequencing was simply ignored.

The first city directory to list street addresses was in 1856, and the numbers often were not correct, many of them failing to correspond to the insurance maps. At one point, the even numbers were on the south side of the street and the odd numbers were on the north. In addition, in an attempt to cure the problems, during the decades the postal numbers were changed several times (e.g., 1895–1896). Today all these factors create problems when researching the buildings on Queen Street.

When examining the directories and maps, it is sometimes impossible to determine whether the occupants resided in an original structure or one that has been replaced or enlarged. Consulting the property assessment rolls is of dubious help, because the street numbers changed frequently. Adding to the problem, building permits are only available in the archives from 1882 onward, and today, many of the stores on Queen Street have no visible postal numbers.

Despite the litany of excuses listed above, any errors that have occurred in this study are my own, and I accept responsibility.

Visiting the Buildings Located on Today's Queen Street (between Spadina and University Avenues)

The best view of the buildings on the south side of Queen Street is from the north sidewalk, and similarly the north side is best seen from the south. This allows one to examine the upper floors, where the architectural history is most evident. However, this entails walking the strip twice, once in each direction. Strolling on the south side is pleasing in hot weather, but in Toronto, long winters are the norm. Even in spring and autumn, people prefer walking in the sunshine, so they tend to walk on the north side of the street.

As a result, in this study I have described the buildings in the order in which they are encountered when walking eastward from Spadina Avenue, regardless of whether they are on the north or the south side of the street.

The Northeast Corner of Spadina Avenue and Queen Street West

This large intersection is one of the busiest in the city. This was true a century and a half ago and remains so today. During the 1850s, Spadina Avenue commenced at Queen Street and stretched northward to the home of William Baldwin (1775–1844), on the heights north of Davenport Road. The section of Spadina south of Queen was named Brock Street, as a tribute to Major-General Sir Isaac Brock, the British general and hero of the War of 1812. Spadina was an impressive thoroughfare, 132 feet wide, deriving its name from Baldwin's home high on the hill. Today, Spadina remains one of the widest avenues in Toronto.

On the south side of Queen, a few doors west of Spadina, near McDougall's Lane, was the home of James Fitzgibbon. During the War of 1812, Laura Secord carried a message at night through enemy lines to warn Fitzgibbon about the impending American attack. The following day at Beaver Dams, Fitzgibbon was successful in forcing the enemy to yield.

In 1819, a census listed that Fitzgibbon resided on Queen Street, with his wife and six children. One of his sons and two of his daughters were over sixteen, while two of the boys and one girl were under sixteen.

During the troubled times that culminated in the 1837 Rebellion, it was Fitzgibbon who saved William Lyon Mackenzie from being attacked by a mob. A few month later, Fitzgibbon led the militia north up Yonge Street to disperse the rebels who had gathered at Montgomery's Tavern. However, in later years, despite repeated attempts for financial compensation for his efforts on behalf of the colony, he was denied any real monetary assistance. Almost penniless, he resided in his house on Queen Street near Spadina. Eventually he returned to England and lived out his final years in a small cottage on the grounds of Windsor Castle.

Henry Scadding visited him there and reported that Fitzgibbon was a broken man. He stated that Fitzgibbon eagerly scanned Canadian newspapers when they arrived in the mail. Despite being so distant from Toronto, his heart remained in the city. The corner of Spadina and Queen was only a two-minute walk from his former home, and was likely the intersection that remained most vividly in his memories. Today, the sight of the street corner would be beyond his imagination.

Queen Street on the east side of Spadina is ninety feet wide. Today, restaurants and pubs take advantage of the spacious sidewalk to locate outdoor patios. Crowds, consisting mostly of young people, gather to enjoy the many entertainers—musicians, drummers, mimes, jugglers, flame-throwers, artists, and sidewalk painters. Vendors sell jewellery, pottery, and self-published books. A student with a megaphone preaches the virtues of a certain political viewpoint or faith. The street is a collage of colour and diversified activity.

The section of Queen Street east of Spadina was planned as an impressive approach leading from Spadina eastward to Maria Street (now Soho Street). At the top of this street was Petersfield, the spacious home of Peter Russell, the administrator of the colony who assumed the reins of power after Governor Simcoe returned to England. Petersfield was eventually demolished, but its owner's name remains (Peter Street) and the extra width of the street still exists today.

The corner of Queen Street West and Spadina Avenue, looking north, on September 29, 1910.

City of Toronto Archives, Fonds 1231, File 231, Item 2046

378 Queen Street West

Bank building at the northeast corner of Spadina and Queen Streets

During the early 1840s, a modest wood-frame house was built on this site, which later became a small hotel. In 1856, its proprietor was Henry McEvoy, who operated a tavern and grocery business. In 1864, John Clark became the tavern-keeper. Throughout the years, it changed ownership several more times. At one time it was named Brown's Hotel; then it became Brewer's Hotel. It became the Avenue Hotel in 1880, but it remained under the management of Mr. J. Brewer, the former proprietor. In 1888, the building was vacant.

In 1902, the Bank of Hamilton purchased the property. The bank also bought the three shops to the east on Queen Street, giving them possession of the buildings from 380 (at the corner) to 374. These were all demolished, and an impressive building was erected, which remains on the site today. It was given the postal number 378. The Bank of Hamilton's architect was G. W. Gouinlock, who designed an ornate red-brick building with limestone trim and a stone façade on the ground-floor level.

For customer convenience, the door was angled so that it was accessible from both Spadina and Queen Streets. Pilasters decorate either side of the entranceway. Above the doorway the architect placed a faux balcony containing pillar-like railings, with ornate curled brackets for support. In the cornice there are dentils and under the eaves there are modillions, with cement keystones above the windows on the second floor.

In 1925, the Bank of Commerce purchased the property and opened a branch. This eventually changed names when the Bank of Commerce and the Imperial Bank of Canada merged to become the Canadian Imperial Bank of Commerce, known today as the CIBC.

Today, some might consider the bank too ornate due to its excess of decorative detail. However, in the era it was built, its architecture was considered attractive and it was very much appreciated. The quality of the workmanship was of the highest calibre, putting to shame many of the modern structures that have been constructed in downtown Toronto. The bank's architecture attempted to impress customers by presenting a solid and prosperous appearance, thus inspiring confidence in the bank.

The ornate Bank of Hamilton Building, constructed in 1902, on the northeast corner of Spadina Avenue and Queen Street.

441–443 Queen Street West

Southeast corner of Spadina Avenue and Queen Street, ornate tower with pointed roof

In 1858, a small house occupied this site, while the two lots to the east were vacant. In 1886, the dwelling was demolished and an ornate building, designed by Langley and Burke, was erected, which opened as the dry goods store of the Devaney brothers. It is a three-storey, red-brick structure with a wide wood cornice at the top, and above the first floor level the trim contains dentils. The rectangular windows allowed maximum amount of light to enter the interior. The gabled windows closest to the corner of the building are ornamented with more wood trim than the others. At the corner of the building, on the first-floor level, the supporting limestone pillar is corroded. It possesses a steel support.

The impressive tower was a landmark for many decades, and today it is in a good state of repair. The architectural treasure defines the intersection. Every time I walk past it, I gaze up at its unique outline. It always retains its distinctive charm, whether it is capped with snow or is baking under the summer sun.

During the 1980s, artists rented rooms on the second and third levels as studio space. The location was near the Ontario College of Art (OCAD), and close to the modestly-priced restaurants of Queen Street. On evenings when funds were scarce, the Spadina Hotel was only a few blocks south. In the friendly pub-style atmosphere on the second floor, they could commiserate with aspiring artists who considered the Toronto art scene staid and unable to accept newer, fresher approaches. For those who had sold a piece of art, a meal at Le Select Bistro was a modest way to celebrate.

Eventually, rental prices became too expensive and the artists relocated further west along Queen Street, where rents were cheaper. One of the artists, who rented space in this building at the corner of Queen and Spadina, now teaches at the University of Toronto. It is gratifying to know that the talents of some of the aspiring young artists were eventually recognized.

This photograph of Queen Street West is dated September 29, 1910. In the foreground (on the right-hand side) is the Auditorium Theatre, with what appears to be a penny gum or candy machine attached to the wall. The view is looking east toward Spadina Avenue. The ornate building on the southeast corner of Spadina and Queen (441–443 Queen) is visible.

City of Toronto Archives, Fonds 1231, File 1231, Item 761

439 Queen Street West

South side, next door to the corner building, on the east side

In 1862, this was butcher shop and grocery store, and in 1864, it became a tavern. In 1870, Samuel Bartlett, a carpenter, occupied the site, and in 1878, it was the hardware store of William Martin. By 1884, it became the

Toronto Co-Operative Association, which had seven locations throughout the city. On this site there was a shop marketing dry goods and groceries. It was a steam laundry in 1890.

The passage of time has not been kind to this three-storey, red-brick building. The two dormer windows in the roof on the top floor reveal the age of the structure. The chimney on the east side was removed, but the one on the west survives. Examining the east wall, one can see the original red brick, and it is evident that the bricks in the peak have been replaced.

Typical of many structures on the street, the upper floors were originally living space for a family, while the first floor was a retail shop or some other commercial enterprise. The modern era ignores the history of the building, placing garish signs over much of the façade, thus hiding the old brick and second-floor windows.

Building on the corner on the southeast corner of Spadina Avenue and Queen Street West (441–443 Queen), with 439 Queen Street to the east of it (left-hand side).

372–366 Queen Street West
North side of street, east of the bank building

In the 1850s, the entire block along Queen Street, from Spadina east to Soho Street, was a row of small houses, known as the Petersfield Row. Their name was derived from the estate of Peter Russell, which was at the north end of Soho Street, a short distance from Queen Street.

Today, located immediately to the east of the bank building, there are three small buildings, their dormers in the roofs overlooking the street. It is difficult to ascertain if these are the remnants of the former small homes, built over and modified, or if they are new structures. If the buildings are original, the old houses are obscured by modern storefronts.

The original houses did not appear on the city map of 1842, but they were on an 1858 map. In 1856, the first Toronto directory was published, which listed the streets and postal addresses. Prior to this year, only the names of the occupants were given, listed in alphabetical order, with their addresses appearing after the names. They likely constructed the original small row houses on this site on Queen Street between the years 1851 and 1856. During the years 1856 and 1880, they were converted into shops, with the second floor and attic spaces in most instances becoming residential quarters, similar to today.

Small shops with addresses 372-366 Queen Street West.

352 Queen Street—Sidewalk Plaques
Honouring those authors who have won City of Toronto Book Awards

Until 2004, every September the section of Queen Street West between University and Spadina avenues was the site of the largest outdoor book festival in Canada: The Word on the Street. Since 1973, the Authors' Walk of Fame has honoured the winners of the Toronto Book Awards, which recognized literary excellence that reflected the life of the city. In the sidewalk (on the north side of the street) in front of 356 Queen Street, their names have been placed—William Kurelick, Timothy Findley, Morley Callaghan, and Margaret Atwood. In all, there are seven blocks of black stone, containing the many names. The final one was inscribed in 1994.

On the last Sunday in September, to accommodate the festival, the street was closed to vehicle traffic and the streetcars were rerouted, allowing visitors to stroll among the hundreds of kiosks and stalls to examine a myriad of published and unpublished writing. Unknown authors displayed their latest desktop musings, while famous writers read aloud to an enthralled public. There were exhibits for children and science-fiction buffs, as well for those who sought mystery, romance, or history.

Restaurants and food stands offered exotic treats, infusing the air with the aromatic bouquet of spices, familiar and otherwise. Canvas tents with colourful posters and pennants created the mediaeval atmosphere of a town fair of old Europe. It was an event worthy of attending. It was uniquely Canadian, but multicultural and international in scope.

In September of 2004, because the event had outgrown its Queen Street location, they relocated it to Queen's Park.

356–342 Queen Street West
Row of three-storey, red-brick buildings that comprise eight shops

Originally, small houses occupied the site of these impressive buildings, a part of the Petersfield Row, which extended from Spadina to Soho Street. The houses on this site were demolished in the 1880s because the city had grown considerably, causing land prices to inflate and necessitating more spacious structures be constructed to accommodate the increase in commercial activity. There was no extra space available on Queen Street, so the only alternative was to build higher and extend further back, thus creating a row of tall, narrow buildings.

In 1888 nine three-storey buildings were built, numbers 358 to 342 Queen Street. They named them the Noble Block, after Mrs. Emma Noble, a widow who owned the land on which seven of the buildings were to be located and who provided the funds for their construction. She had inherited the land from her father, William Noble, a retired farmer. It was a commercial block with stores on the first-floor level, and residential spaces above. The architectural firm of Smith and Gimmell designed them. The façades were similar in style.

Another widow, Mrs. Mary Ann Harvard, owned the two properties to the immediate west of the Noble property (356–358 Queen Street). She intended to invest with Mrs. Noble and add two more buildings to the block. However, for some unknown reason she opted out of the plan. She sold the land and the new owner did not wish to participate in the scheme. Thus, the two buildings to the west of the Noble Block were not constructed until several years later.

When they were finally constructed, though the colour of the bricks was not the same, they were similar in design, complementing the earlier structures. Today, they have been combined into a single store and have the postal address 356. Even though the paint that has been applied to the bricks is now peeling, they remain impressive. All nine of the structures are excellent examples of late-Victorian commercial architecture.

In the Noble Block, five of the red-brick buildings, numbered 354 to 346, have symmetrical façades, while the two to the east of them, numbers 344 and 342, have large arched windows on the second floor. In all the buildings, the windows are wide and spacious. Some contain coloured glass in the top sections, many with blue glass and a few with green, their designs and patterns being quite attractive. They are surrounded by much ornamental wood trim. Most of the storefronts at the ground floor level have been severely altered and modernized. Numbers 348 and 346 are perhaps the least changed. High in the cornices are dentils and other interesting designs. There are so many shapes and patterns in this row of buildings that each time a person examines the structures, further details are often noted. Listed below are the merchants who were the first occupants of ground-floor shops of the 1888 Noble Block, and the two buildings to the west of the block. From west to east they are as follows:

Occupants of 356-358 (today #356) Queen Street West

358, Albert Harvard, drugs

356, Mr. N. Olives, fruits

Noble Block, 354-346 Queen Street West

354, Fawcett and Peterman, tailors

352, Pearson and Company, hats

350, John W. Clark, barber

348, Archibald Loughrey, cigars

346, Toronto Musical Instrument Company

344–342, Fleming and Company, furniture

356-342 Queen Street West (The Noble Block, constructed 1888).

Row of shops with postal address 425 Queen Street West.

425 Queen Street West

South side of the street, with four modern glass façades with peaks, containing six stores

In the 1850s, where these modern buildings are located, was the property of the McLean sisters. They donated the land to the Methodist church, for the construction of a church. The Wesleyan Methodist Chapel appeared on a map dated 1858, set back a distance from the street. The 1850s was a time when many of the churches were rather puritanical in doctrine, the Methodist Church among them, maintaining a very strict code of behaviour. The wearing of gold jewellery, ornately trimmed clothing, or even flowers in a hat was forbidden. Theatre attendance, dancing, and card-playing were frowned upon. In the mid-nineteenth century, Methodism did not occupy a prestigious position in society, as few of its members were among the professional class and even fewer were wealthy.

W. H. Pearson, in his book *Recollections and Records of Toronto of Old*, (Williams Briggs, Toronto, 1914), wrote: "The proceedings at Methodist services were frequently very similar to the activities which one might witness in many a Negro church in the southern United States today … the exhortation of the minister, the moans of the sinners, and the general emotional excitement."

The Methodist church eventually split over a disagreement of doctrine and formed several different groups: Episcopal, Primitive, and British Wesleyan. The latter was the largest and most important group. Congregations that wished to follow the simple teachings of early-day Methodism became known as the Primitive Methodists. The church on Queen was one of their gathering places. In the 1860s and 1870s, some of the groups reunited, but even as late as 1884, the church on Queen Street near Spadina was referred to as the Primitive Methodist Church. The Methodist church on Queen Street remained until 1922, when it was finally closed. In 1925, the majority of Methodist congregations in Canada amalgamated with several other churches to form the United Church of Canada. The building on Queen Street remained empty until 1926, when it was purchased by another congregation and opened as the Queen City Evangelistic Temple. In 1930, it again changed hands and became the Church of All Nations, which survived until the early 1980s. Its demolition made available a large piece of land fronting Queen Street, thus permitting the construction of the present buildings.

The modern three-storey building with the four peaked roofs is named the Queen & Spadina Business Centre, and is divided into six stores. Its façade of mirrored glass provides an excellent reflection of the historic Noble Block, on the north side of the street.

The Le Select Bistro when it was located on Street West.

328 Queen Street West
East side of The Rivoli, north side of Queen Street

In the 1850s, this property was occupied by a small house, which possessed a shop on the ground-floor level. It was a part of the Petersfield Row and contained a bread and biscuit bakery operated by Richard Reeves. During the years ahead, it became a jewellery store and also a shoe store. In the late 1870s, the old structure was demolished and replaced with a larger building. A city map of 1880 reveals that the new, larger premises housed a bakery, its proprietor being Mr. A. Cureston. The baking ovens were at the rear, away from the street. This is the same building that occupies the site today.

The building on this location extends back considerably. It has three storeys, the red bricks have been painted grey, and the quoins (brick pattern) at the corners possess the same colour. The façade is very plain and contains large rectangular windows. When it was constructed, Canada was in the midst of an economic depression and ornamentation was considered an unnecessary expense. There are four large chimneys, which strangely have yellow bricks rather than red to match the building. The dormer windows in the roof are typical of the 1870s.

The various commercial establishments that have occupied the site at 328 Queen West mirror the various stages in the development of the street. At the beginning of the nineteenth century, the area was a successful middle-class commercial and residential area.

During this period, number 328 was a popular bakery. The scent of fresh bread baking in the large ovens wafted over busy Queen Street. Each morning, six days a week, customers appeared at the door, anxious to purchase their daily supply. Few treats in life surpass the pleasure of warm bread, fresh from a hot oven. When times were difficult, this bakery on Queen Street suffered, as housewives baked their own bread to economize.

As the city expanded, they extended new streetcar lines into the suburbs, and downtown neighbourhoods like Queen West became less favoured as places to live. As well, the area to the south of Queen changed from residential to commercial, and housed the garment industry. The large commercial buildings on Spadina, built mostly in the 1920s, reflected this transition. By the 1950s, the area had become rather shabby. In 1956, 328 Queen Street was one of the locations on Queen Street that was empty and available for rent.

In 1957, Moe's Delicatessen opened on the site, catering to the Jewish workers who were employed in the garment trade. However, Moe's did not last long, closing two years later. Next it became Robbin's Restaurant, but this business remained in operation for less than twelve months. For the next four years the premises were empty. In 1963, Mr. Finley Brown, a doorman at Loew's Theatre at 328 Yonge Street (now the Elgin Theatre), was listed as the sole occupant, likely renting an apartment on one of the upper floors.

Billy Bee's Snack Bar occupied the ground floor in 1964 and 1965. It was replaced in 1966 with the Modern Restaurant, which served Chinese food, Mr. Law Wing being the owner of the business. He was relatively successful and remained on the premises until 1971. The site was empty the next year, but in 1973, Michi Japanese Restaurant opened. This eatery lasted until 1977, when a Parisian-style eatery, Le Select Bistro, appeared. By this time, the area was attracting artists who were seeking inexpensive rental accommodation for studios. The restaurant was soon quite popular with the artistic clientele, as they considered the atmosphere of old Europe to be very appealing.

Le Select Bistro was the result of a partnership between Jean-Jacques Quinsac and Frederick Geissweiller, inspired by a favourite eatery that they had enjoyed in Paris during their student days. It successfully captured the ambiance of a bistro—the art posters, mirrors, and a bar imported from Paris. Typical of such establishments, the tables were relatively small and close together. The wicker bread baskets hanging above each table, suspended from the ceiling with twine, allowed the clientele to lower them when they wanted bread and raise them when not required. This novel idea conserved much needed space on the tables.

In winter, the restaurant was delightfully cozy, and in summer, the doors facing the street opened onto a sidewalk patio, creating a cozy oasis surrounded by greenery amid the busy foot-traffic and clanging of the streetcars. There was an excellent selection of wines, and the fixed-price menu, at one time so typical of the Parisian eateries, was reasonable. It is a pity that this tradition is becoming rarer in the French capital, as food has become extremely expensive in Europe, although this has not deterred the flocks of tourists who flock to the restaurants.

In 2005, Le Select Bistro relocated to Wellington Street, west of Spadina Avenue, four blocks south of Queen Street. The new location has wider sidewalks, and the street has considerably less noise and vehicle traffic. The mature trees and surrounding historic buildings offer a more tranquil atmosphere, where they have again recreated the ambiance of old Paris.

The restaurant maintains its excellent standards of cuisine in its new location. However, I must admit that I miss its cozy Queen Street location, with its intimate patio.

326 Queen Street West
Two doors east of The Rivoli

In the 1850s, this site was occupied by three small houses, similar to its neighbour, a part of the Petersfield Row. During the 1870s, they were demolished and replaced by three larger buildings.

The tall yellow-brick chimneys have survived, and those on the west side retain the nineteenth-century chimney pots, which they inserted to prevent sparks from igniting the roofs of nearby buildings. These were necessary in the days when heat was provided by open fireplaces with crackling flames that often sent showers of sparks skyward. Two of the dormer windows on the roof also remain. Roman arches stand atop the second-floor windows. Each pair of windows shares a common stone sill, and below the sill, simple details enhance the overall design.

At one time, the building housed a branch of the Royal Canadian Legion and was frequented by soldiers of Ukrainian origin. Thus, it was officially known the Ukrainian Legion. It was also home to the Canadian-Ukrainian Committee and the Ukrainian-Canadian Relief Fund. Until 2008, a plaque stood on the wall of the ground floor, to the left of the doorway, commemorating the life of Filip Konowal, who enlisted in the Seventy-seventh Canadian Battalion during the First World War. In August of 1917, he "fought with valour," as the plaque states, near Lens, in France, and on October 15 of the same year, in London, King George V awarded him the Victoria Cross.

The new occupants of the building have removed the plaque.

320 Queen Street West
Small one-storey shop on north side of street

This narrow store is an example of a half-size building lot that remained vacant after the row houses of the Petersfield Row were demolished. In 1878, there was no building on the site, but in 1879, the Toronto directories reveal that Edward De La Hooke, a watchmaker, had opened a shop on the premises, having the postal number 316½. In this decade, it was common for watchmakers to place large clocks in their shop windows to allow those passing on the street to check the accuracy of their pocket watches. It was a free service that they provided to attract attention to their establishments.

Half numbers were common on Queen Street when they erected small structures to infill narrow spaces. In 1884, 316½ was the barbershop of James Bennett, and in 1890, the cigar store of John Adair. Both of these establishments provided a place where men could gather to chat and exchange news as well as argue politics.

The shop is a two-storey building of red brick, although they have painted the bricks yellow. The original cornice at the top, at some unknown time, was removed and replaced with a plain metal trim. The windows on the second floor have also been altered.

Bedo Store
318 Queen Street West

The building to the east of number 320 was at one time among the most imposing structures on the street. Today, it is in need of restoration work, epitomizing the phrase "arrogantly shabby." Its first occupant was James Steel, a tailor. Though "ready-made" suits were becoming more common, most gentlemen with means still preferred to choose the material and have their suits made to order. James Steel catered to the needs of such clients, but he was deferential to anyone purchasing clothes within his fine shop.

Built in the 1880s, this style of architecture was very popular during that decade. It is one of the few Richardsonian Romanesque structures remaining on Queen. It is solid and heavy, similar to a fortress, with large stones employed as lintels above the windows. Its faux-tower inserted into the steeply sloped roof is a reminder of past glories. With three floors plus an attic, it was constructed of red brick that has sadly been painted a dark, dismal grey. A person is left to imagine the appearance of this building if its bricks and stonework were cleaned and restored to display their original mellow yellow and red. This might be said of many of the stores on Queen Street.

View from the Northwest Corner of Soho and Queen Streets

At this corner it is possible to gaze north up the short avenue that today is named Soho Street. In the early days of the town of York, this was the carriageway that entered Petersfield, which was at the north end of the Soho Street of today. Petersfield was on park lot 14, owned by Peter Russell.

Peter Russell was born in Cork, Ireland, in 1731, a member of an English aristocratic family that included the Duke of Bedford. Bedford Road in Toronto was named after Peter Russell's important relative. As a young man, Russell decided to pursue a career within the church and enrolled in religious studies at Cambridge University. Before he was able to complete his degree, he was forced to resign because of gambling debts. As a result, he purchased a commission in the British Army and served in the American Revolutionary War, and they appointed him as the civilian secretary to the British commander-in-chief. During these years, he also became acquainted with John Graves Simcoe.

At the end of the war, Russell returned to England to find that his prospects were not too promising. He sold his military commission to raise funds to support his father and sister, Elizabeth. When Simcoe was appointed lieutenant governor of Upper Canada in 1791, he persuaded Russell to sail to North America and promised him the appointment of receiver general of the province. Peter Russell accepted, and the following year he immigrated to Canada and settled at Niagara-on-the-Lake. Along with the position of receiver general, he also became a member of the legislative and executive councils. He stood beside Simcoe when the first Parliamentary session of Upper Canada was held at Niagara, out of doors under an enormous oak tree.

In 1793, when Simcoe relocated the capital of the colony to Toronto, he granted Russell ownership to a small piece of property within the newly planned town. In that day, the town was located at the eastern end of the harbour. It was a choice lot overlooking the cool water of the lake, at the corner of today's Front and Princess Streets. Here he built a fine home and named it Russell Abbey.

Because Russell was a bachelor, his sister, Elizabeth, who was also unmarried, kept house for him. They were among the more influential citizens of York, both socially and politically. This was the beginning of the group that in later years became known as the Family Compact.

When personages such as Peter Russell were granted title to land within the town, they also received park lots to provide income, and in some instances sites for country homes. Simcoe granted park lot 14 to Peter Russell. It extended from today's Huron Street to Beverley Street. On it, Russell built a country home and named it after himself, Petersfield. It was located beside a stream, named Russell Creek, on some maps listed as Russell's Creek. In December of 1805, his estate manager advertised in *The Oracle* that potatoes from Petersfield were for sale, the minimum purchase to be not less than ten bushels.

In the early 1800s, he purchased park lot 15, which gave him possession of all the land on the north side of Queen Street (Lot Street) between Beverley Street and Spadina Avenue. He also gained title to park lot 16, west of Spadina.

Today, a painting of Peter Russell is in the Baldwin Collection at the Toronto Reference Library. It depicts a portly older man, bearing a resemblance to Thomas Jefferson. It was said that Russell was a person of forceful character. His letters reveal that to his superiors he was extremely deferential. He was also accused of having a prodigious proclivity for acquiring titles.

One historian joked that he would have been a wonderful character to include in a Gilbert and Sullivan opera, such as *The Mikado*. Some felt that he was a well-qualified receiver-general, as he was always "receiving." He acquired much property, sometimes by granting it to himself, thus becoming a very wealthy man.

On September 30, 1808, Peter Russell died at Russell Abbey, his home within the old town of York. Lieutenant-Governor Gore was the chief mourner, and Reverent Stuart conducted the service, with the military honours provided by the Garrison Commander of Fort York, Major Fuller. The ownership of Petersfield passed to Elizabeth Russell, Peter Russell's sister.

Records do not state the year that they demolished Petersfield, but Henry Scadding reported that it remained in existence in 1872. He wrote that as a boy he remembered "the homely coziness [of Petersfield] whose interior was lighted up by a rousing hospitable fire of great logs, piled high in one of the usual capacious and lofty fireplaces of the time." (*Toronto of Old,* Henry Scadding, Toronto, Oxford University Press, 1966)

It is a pity that this historic home was lost to future generations. Much of Toronto's past has disappeared in this manner.

**298 Queen Street, at the northeast corner
of Soho and Queen Streets.**

The Black Bull

298 Queen Street West, northeast corner of Soho and Queen Streets

The sign attached to the south side of the building states that the tavern was established in 1822. However, in that year, it was a modest wood-frame two-storey building with a steep-pitched roof. The doorway was at the corner of the premises, allowing patrons to enter from either Queen or Soho Streets.

In 1861, the owner added a mansard roof. During this year, patrons in the pub hotly debated the merits of confederation with the other North American British colonies. In 1885, they added an extension on the north side, on Soho Street. This was the year of the Northwest Rebellion, when Sir John A. Macdonald sent troops to the west. In 1910, they again extensively renovated the Black Bull, employing brick cladding to encase the entire building. In this year, King Edward VII died. He had been the most popular British monarch since the mid-seventeenth century.

Today, the pub is an attractive Second Empire–style building of red brick, with yellow-brick pilasters on the west side. The main door, which at one time was at the corner, has been moved to the Queen Street side of the tavern. The slate-rock tiles on the roof have survived, but they are painted yellow.

Attached to the north end of the Black Bull, 2 Soho Street, is a house that matches the brickwork of the hotel. Its simple, cohesive design has heavy stone blocks and Roman arches above the windows, in the Richardsonian Romanesque style.

321 Queen Street West
Southwest corner of Queen and Peter Streets

In 1891, on this corner was a hotel named Middleton House, owned by Samuel Hunter. It was constructed on a 26-by-109-foot building lot and was assessed at $7150. Its exterior was roughcast, consisting of a plaster surface of lime, cement, sand, and gravel. The proprietor was Leonard J. Hewitt, age fifty-one. He and his wife Catherine had three children.

In 1880, Hunter renamed it the Toronto House. When the building was enlarged and a third floor added, it is not known if the original structure was included in the newer building or demolished. In 1910, it was listed as the Royal Edward Hotel, and it remained in operation until 1930, when the records reveal that the building was vacant. Today, it is a commercial retail property.

**373 Queen Street, at the southeast corner of
Queen and Peter Street, August 2009.**

373 Queen Street West

Southeast corner of Peter and Queen Streets

In 1885, this was the grocery shop of R. H. Shepherd, but the premises were vacant in 1890. In 1891, R. Tuthill opened a drug store. The shop contained shelves that reached to the ceiling, the glass jars filled with various concoctions and cures. On the long counter sat more glass containers that the druggist had filled with penny candy, the peppermints and humbugs being among the favourites. At least one jar contained liquorice candy.

It was an era devoid of medical insurance or government plans, so the druggist provided advice and dispensed patent medicines. People only consulted a doctor if the illness was serious, as for most families a doctor's fee was a large financial burden given their frugal weekly budget.

Mr. Tuthill's shop is long gone, but the building has survived into the modern era, its detailed brickwork and Roman-arched windows retaining the charming atmosphere of yesteryear. Inside, on the first floor, is a rolled-tin ceiling. It is worthwhile glancing into the window to view the interior of this fine building.

Queen Street West on June 20, 1912, looking east from the southeast corner of Peter Street. The ornate building at 280 Queen Street, where the sidewalk narrows, is clearly visible. Vehicle traffic is sparse, though the streetcars and the horse and buggy cause the child in the sailor suit to look carefully before crossing the street.

City of Toronto Archives, Fonds 1231, Item 1671

The Silver Snail
367 Queen Street West, south side

In 1890, this Second Empire building was the clothing store of George Adams. The third-floor mansard roof has ornately trimmed windows, and the roof retains the old slate-rock tiles. The brickwork on the west side reveals that the third floor was added later, and was not a part of the original building.

The structure has been altered greatly. The second-floor windows have been filled in with cement blocks, while the first floor has been renovated to suit the needs of modern retailing. In the interior, the crown moulding and rolled-tin ceiling survive.

When my nephews were young boys, they considered the Silver Snail's collection of classic edition comic books to be one of the great wonders of the world. At the time, I wondered how they would view one of the real

"Seven Wonders of the Modern World." I eventually discovered the answer. When they visited Niagara Falls, one of the real seven wonders, they saw it as "just a lot of water." However, they considered a 1940s edition of a Superman comic as a wonder to be truly treasured.

280 Queen Street West

Located on the north side of the street, this impressive building is positioned where the sidewalk narrows. The Canadian television series "*Street Legal*" (a CBC production that ran from1987 to 1994) used exterior shots of the building to represent the offices of the legal team featured in the program.

In 1881, it was Mara's Grocery and Liquor Store. It has been well maintained, and today it appears much as it did in the nineteenth century.

The architecture is highly detailed, with many designs, patterns, and carvings. The three-storey building has large dormer windows on the third floor. It has a mansard roof and an impressive tower.

280 Queen Street West.

299 Queen Street West in 1919, at the southeast corner of John and Queen Streets.

City of Toronto Archives, Fonds 1231, Sub-Series 1231, Item 761

299 Queen Street West
Southeast corner of Queen and John streets

The five-storey white "Industrial Gothic" building occupies the site that was once a part of the estate John Beverley Robinson, and his son Christopher Robinson, born in York (Toronto) in 1828.

Christopher Robinson was educated at Upper Canada College and became a lawyer in 1850. He co-authored a four-volume text on constitutional law, the first text of its type in Canada. He represented the

Crown in the appeal of the murderer of Thomas D'Arcy McGee, who was assassinated in Ottawa. Robinson won the case, and the murderer was hanged. Robinson was also the senior counsel for the Crown in the famous trial of Louis Riel in Regina in 1885. Robinson was again successful, and they executed Riel. Robinson died in 1905.

The Methodist Church eventually purchased Robinson's property to construct a building for its administrative offices and printing enterprises. The architectural firm of Burke, Harwood, and White designed the building in 1913. Construction began in 1914, and when completed was named The Wesley Building, in honour of John Wesley, the founder of Methodism. It eventually became the United Church Publishing House.

The skeleton of the symmetrical building is of steel. The white terra cotta precast cladding tiles contain symbols and "bits and pieces" inspired by the stone traceries in the windows of the Gothic cathedrals of Europe. Quatrefoils abound throughout the exuberant designs. Above the pilasters, at the second-floor level, are the "men of learning," some holding books in their hands. Pinnacles grace the top of the structure. There are crowns above the ornate doorway, as well as lamps, representing the light of knowledge.

A five-year heritage preservation project has restored the façades of the building, and it appears as magnificent as when it was originally built.

On hot summer evenings, when Queen Street is seething with revellers, I sometimes dine at the intimate HoSu Japanese-Korean restaurant across the road from this architectural wonder. When I depart the restaurant, I always gaze across the street at its magnificent floodlit façade. The bright lights accent the tile-work, creating glaring highlights and soft shadows, and I marvel at the artisanship of its builders. They have long since vanished from the scene, but the architectural heritage they bequeathed to the city remains for us to enjoy and appreciate.

Building at the Northeast Corner of John and Queen Street West (coffee shop)

In 1890, this three-storey building with a mansard roof was the bakery of John Tasker. It contains six large gable windows, and the roof shingles have a fish-scale pattern. It is constructed of red bricks, with yellow-brick trim and quoins. The old shop windows have disappeared and the first floor has been entirely modernized.

Building on the northeast corner of John and Queen Streets.

John Street in 1909, looking north from Queen Street toward the Grange (the historic home that is now part of the Art Gallery of Ontario). The slender spire of the Church of St. George the Martyr is on the east (right-hand) side of the roadway. The church, built in 1845, was destroyed by fire in 1955. Only the tower (without the graceful spire atop it) remains today.

City of Toronto Archives, Fonds 1244, Item 2162

242 Queen Street West

This building is a classic example of the structures built on narrow lots, where small houses had previously been located.

In 1864, in a small house on the site, George Price, a merchant, occupied the ground-floor level, and on the second floor was the office of Doctor William Ogden. By 1872, Dr. Ogden occupied the entire building, and his son Albert, a "student-at-law," lived with him. In 1876, Joseph Gates, a wheelwright, lived on the premises.

In 1881, the small two-storey shop was demolished, and the three-storey building you see before you today was erected. Mrs. McNichol operated a dressmaker's shop on the ground floor and lived on the second floor with her husband, a commercial traveller (salesman). The business was not successful, and in 1882, William Barber opened a grocery store on the site. He continued to operate the business until 1907.

After Mr. Barber retired, several merchants attempted to operate businesses, but none lasted very long. In 1913, Jacob Stein opened a men's clothing shop to sell "men's furnishings" to the families and businessmen of the area. Jacob Stein passed away in 1920, and his wife, Dora, continued the business until 1928, when she sold the shop to Esther Miller.

The narrow building possesses a tall parapet (wall) at the top. This was a common architectural feature during the decade, as it gave the appearance of a more impressive façade, even though the parapet had nothing behind it. In the parapet can be seen the year the building was constructed (1881), and a stone railing that simulates a balcony. In the arc at the peak is a sunburst pattern, a simple adornment. The third-storey windows are Roman arches, while those on the second storey are rectangular.

242 Queen Street West.

The City (St. Patrick's) Market
238 Queen Street West

In 1836, Mr. D'Arcy Boulton (1785–1846), who resided at the Grange, donated land on Queen Street to provide a site for a public market. It was Toronto's second market, after the St. Lawrence Market. The property was originally a part of the hundred acre park lot 13, bounded by Queen Street, McCaul, Dundas, and Beverley. The city erected a frame building to protect shoppers from the elements, which they eventually replaced with a modest brick building, completed in 1856. Three prominent citizens provided the funds for the structure, on condition that they would be reimbursed from the profits of the market. The Toronto directories list four butchers as having stalls in the building in 1861. It was destroyed by fire.

The market never became as important as the St. Lawrence or St. Andrew's Market, but it was important to those who resided within walking distance of its stalls. The present-day building dates from 1912, and though it contains fast-food stalls, it awaits a revival to return it to its rightful place as an important shopping venue of Queen Street West.

210–206 Queen Street West.

210–206 Queen Street West

These charming Second Empire–style shops have been joined to create a single commercial space, which today is a restaurant. The slate tiles on the front of the sloped mansard roof remain. Originally, a gable window was above each shop. The three-storey, red-brick shops have simple decorations on the façade, and the tall windows of the original shops survive, although they have been modernized.

In 1890, the most westerly of the shops (210) was the grocery store of Charles Woolnough. The centre shop (208) was the locksmith store of Benjamin Ibbotson. The shop on the east (206) was the confectionary of "Patterson and Wilson."

**194 Queen Street, northeast corner of
Queen and St. Patrick's Streets.**

194 Queen Street West

In 1890, this hotel, on the northeast corner of Queen and St. Patrick's Streets was Williams Hotel, operated by Thomas R. Williams. In that year, it was a two-storey building. The postal address was 196, and St. Patrick's Street on the west side of it was named William Street. In 1891, Owen Cosgrove purchased the property, and renamed it the Angus Kerr Hotel.

Mr. Cosgrove added a third storey to the structure, as well as a narrow pointed parapet in the central position at the top. It was on a building lot that measured 50 by 82 feet, and the land and building, in 1891, had an assessed value of $16,000. The façade is of red bricks, with yellow-brick trim. The first-floor façade has been modernized, and the bricks on the west side covered over. Beneath the windows on the third floor (front) are sandstone lintels.

Shops on the south side of Queen Street, west of Simcoe Street, on August 23, 1931. The historic shop that today has the postal number 225 is the fourth building from the left. The three shops to the east of it have since been demolished.

City of Toronto Archive, Series 372, Sub-Series 3, Item 1234

225 Queen Street West
Small shop on south side, west of parking lot

This shop is one of the oldest structures on the entire street. It was built between the years 1856 and 1861. The houses to the east of it have been demolished to create a parking lot and to provide a site for a bank. It is an excellent example of the small buildings that were constructed during the 1850s and 1860s, with a shop on the first floor and space above it for living quarters. The Toronto directories list dressmakers, waiters, a shoemaker, and grocers as occupants of the small shops in this row.

The bank at the southwest corner of Simcoe and Queen
Streets, on August 23, 1931. In this 1931 photo, the two
shops on the west side of the bank have been demolished.
Today, three more of the shops have disappeared.

City of Toronto Archives, Series 372, Sub-Series 3, Item 1233

Bank on the Southwest Corner of Queen and Simcoe Streets

This fine building was erected in 1930, on the site of a small structure
that once housed the Harris Hotel. The bank resembles a Greek temple,
with its classical designs and two large Ionic columns on either side of
the impressive entrance. The façades at the front and on the west side are
limestone. Above the doorway is a design that incorporates the Greek key.
The west wall is of yellow bricks, with limestone quoins at the northwest
corner. The cornice at the top is of copper, with designs jutting up at either
end and in the central position.

The north side of Queen Street in 1926, between Simcoe
Street on the west and University Avenue on the east. On the
right-hand side of the picture, Osgoode Hall is visible. The
shops were all demolished to provide green space for the Art
Deco Canada Life Building on University Avenue. In 1972,
the insurance company generously donated the land to allow
them to relocate historic Campbell House to the site.

City of Toronto Archives, Fonds 1244, Item 2468

Campbell House in the centre of University Avenue, as it is being moved north to Queen Street in 1972. The house was being relocated from Adelaide Street, to its present-day location.

City of Toronto Archives, Fonds 124, File 2, id0148

Campbell House

160 Queen Street West, Northwest Corner of University Avenue and Queen Street West

This 1822 home was originally on Adelaide Street, near Frederick Street. It was relocated to its present site in 1972. It was the home of Sir William Campbell (1758–1834), sixth chief justice of Ontario.

Born in Caithess, Scotland, Campbell fought in the American Revolution and was a prisoner in Yorktown, Virginia, in 1781. After the war, he settled in Nova Scotia, where he practised law. In 1811, he moved to Upper Canada (Ontario). He was appointed to the King's Bench as a judge, and in 1825, he was Speaker of the Legislative Council of Upper Canada. In 1829, he was knighted, the first such honour bestowed on a member of the judiciary in Upper Canada.

The neo-classical home, with its nine windows in the façade, has been faithfully restored. Its impressive appearance reflects the important position Campbell held in the town of York. It is of red brick, on a stone foundation. Four Ionic pillars support the graceful porch that protects the doorway, with its fanned-shaped transom window and small sidelight panes of glass. The triangular pediment is a classical Greek design.

The 1821 home of Sir William Campbell at 160 Queen Street West.

Conclusion

Today, some of the oldest communities in Toronto are becoming the newest residential districts in the city. All these areas are on the verge of "becoming," unlike urban areas that have already "become," where future possibilities are limited.

In the early nineteenth century, the King-Spadina area was a thriving residential community with numerous small shops. During the latter years of the century and the early decades of the twentieth century, due to the demands of industry and changing economic conditions, the district evolved into a hive of industry and commerce. In the 1990s, when the city changed its bylaws, they allowed owners to employ the industrial buildings for multiple purposes. The Kings West District was reborn. During the next few years, the area continued to transform. The trend accelerated as more companies relocated to the suburbs.

By the dawn of the twenty-first century, many of the empty loft-style warehouses had been converted into much sought-after offices, attracting creative industries that required flexible spacing. Many of the clubs and restaurants of the Entertainment District are now housed in the old buildings east of Spadina, and along King Street to the west. The proximity of the city's cultural institutions and the restaurants drew people to the areas as places to live, and once more, the streets became residential. Condominiums appeared along the avenues. More restaurants, boutiques, and shops opened to respond to the needs of the residents.

Other areas of the city also changed. The Jewish Kensington Market emerged as a home for the stores of many ethnic groups. Queen Street West, dilapidated in the 1960s, finally emerged as a trendy district, a desirable locations for shops, boutiques, and restaurants. The St. Andrew's Playground, which had been sadly neglected, received a facelift. Gardens and paved walkways restored the charm of yesteryear. In 2009, the St. Andrew's Market of old was re-established.

It is hoped that during the years ahead, as the streets and buildings of Toronto continue to be transformed, the history of these historic areas will continue to be appreciated and maintained, so that city's "Villages Within" will never disappear from the urban scene.